MW00460198

"*Millennials' Guide to Relationships* provides a one-stop action-able workbook for the minefields of the myriad relationships a generation juggling outsize expectations, a difficult world, and re-defined paradigms about love, family, and work are managing. The beauty of this book is that it can be tailored to the relationship needs of the reader — whether it's dating, family issues, or roommates. Drs. Hallett and Wisdom do a great job of consistently revisiting the pillars of healthy relationships such as self-reflection, self-awareness, respect, and empathy, qualities that can often get lost in the shuffle."

— **Ramani Durvasula**, PhD, Clinical Psychologist, Professor of Psychology, and Author

"*Millennials' Guide to Relationships* is full of down-to-earth tips for people at any stage in life. If you are a person who sometimes speaks to other people, this lists reasonable, objective advice based on your situation and what you want for yourself—not what society or the authors think you should be doing."

— **Caroline Mays**, English Professor and admitted Millennial

"*Millennials' Guide to Relationships* is another must-have Millennials' guide for your bookshelf, providing clear and action-oriented guidance for people in their 20's and 30's who are looking to build and strengthen existing relationships. The book is easy to navigate and offers quick yet thorough considerations, tips, and tricks that can be applied to romantic, professional, familial and other relationships. *Millennials' Guide to Relationships* will be a helpful resource for Millennials to use in their own lives and for them to share with friends, family, and other loved ones of all ages."

— **Jennifer Felner**, PhD, San Diego, CA

"Dr. Hallett and Dr. Wisdom's guide to relationships is extremely helpful for anyone, but especially a Millennial such as myself – it's like having a therapist and a best friend in your back pocket! I will be recommending this incredible resource to all Millennial clients I work with as an occupational therapist as well as to all my friends!"

— **Laura Stursberg**, Occupational Therapy Doctoral Student

"*Millennials' Guide to Relationships* is a wonderful breakdown of how to look at your feelings, figure out your intentions, and interact with other humans to have a successful relationship with yourself, your friends, your family, and even romantically. I really enjoyed the road map-style reading and feel like I gained a lot of knowledge and tools on how to have healthier relationships. This book has so much useful information and it is written in a manner which is easy to digest and fun to read."

— **Leah Gallagher-Hull**, Real Life Millennial

"*Millennials' Guide to Relationships* is one of the most powerful guides to navigating any relationship. The candid and direct support given by Dr. Kristina Hallett and Dr. Jennifer Wisdom is gold. If and when you ever struggle no matter what kind of relationship it may be, this book will guide you to the other side with care and honesty."

— **Tricia Brouk**, Director, Writer, Producer, Curator, Coach

MILLENNIALS' GUIDE TO RELATIONSHIPS

Happy And Healthy Relationships
Are Not a Myth!

Greg - Thanks so much for everything! Wishing you happy + healthy relationships!

Jennifer Wisdom

WINDING PATHWAY BOOKS

KRISTINA HALLETT, PhD ABPP

JENNIFER P. WISDOM, PhD MPH ABPP

Published by Winding Pathway Books

WINDING PATHWAY BOOKS

ISBN (print): 978-1-954374-00-3
ISBN (e-book): 978-1-954374-01-0

Book design by: Deana Riddle at Bookstarter
Cover design by Brian Sisco at 115 Studios and Diego G. Diaz
Photo credit: Diego G. Diaz

For more information or bulk orders, visit: www.leadwithwisdom.com

Printed in the United States of America

Acknowledgements

We wish to thank the following for their expert and insightful comments: Lindsay Harris, Jennifer Felner, Alison Feuer, Adam Hart, Maria Lawrence, Greg Muriello, Laura Stursberg, and Elizabeth Warren. We appreciate Diego G. Diaz for cover design and photography, Deana Riddle at Bookstarter for publishing support, and Cassandra Blake for exemplary administrative assistance.

Table of Contents

PART 3. RELATIONSHIP WITH ROMANTIC PARTNERS

How to Use this Book

This is not a book best read cover to cover. We encourage you to review the table of contents and identify a challenge you are currently having or recently experienced. Turn to those pages to start finding a solution!

This book is about relationships — all of the different types of relationships that we may have, including the relationship with yourself! Each challenge includes a brief description and a number of possible solutions that you may want to try. Many times, you can see success after trying just one option. You'll see some solutions repeated across different challenges because they're likely to be helpful for many problems. For complex challenges, you may want to attempt several interventions at the same time. We suggest using a little bit of the scientific method as you try this process: After you identify the challenge you're having, visualize what it would look like for you once the issue is resolved. Then as you try out solutions, you have an ideal to measure progress against. It's helpful if you take an approach of curiosity; pretend you're Sherlock Holmes trying to figure out and solve the problem, or putting together a massive 3-D puzzle.

It's important to have patience and give the solutions a little bit of time to work. Some ideas that you try won't solve the problem but will make it a little better — that's still success! If you don't feel comfortable trying a solution or if it works partially or not at all, try something else. Some of the solutions are very low risk, such as changing your expectations of the other person. Others can appear more challenging, such as directly discussing a concern with a partner or asking your roommate to move out. Start with solutions that feel lower risk to you and work your way up to more challenging solutions.

It's important to remember a few basic rules of relationships that will never steer you wrong:

1. Be honest *and* diplomatic with everyone, including yourself.

2. Listen to what others are saying before responding.

3. Be patient. Sometimes people are working on your behalf to make things better and you don't even know it.

4. Be curious about yourself and seek constant self-improvement.

5. Set and maintain boundaries and limits that reflect your priorities within your relationship(s).

6. Remember that we all have struggles. Be kind and respectful.

As you work through possible solutions, you'll get better at knowing yourself, reading situations, responding to issues, building relationships, and applying solutions effectively. There will sometimes be situations in which there is a game being played around you that you don't fully get — a version of "relationship politics". Observe, be patient, clarify your own boundaries, and learn. The more you know what you want, the more you'll be able to achieve your goals and have the kind of relationships you want. If you're not sure what you want, that's okay too — that's a perfect place to be while you're in your 20s and 30s. The goal of the strategies in this book is to help you develop skills that will serve you well as you continue to move forward in life.

Each of you reading this book is a unique person with talents to share with the world. Our hope is that this book can make it easier for you to do so. Good luck improving your relationships!

Part 1.
Who are you? Getting to Know Yourself

Challenge 1.
Knowing What You Like

In order to have positive relationships (including family, friendships, professional colleagues and intimate partners), it really helps to have a sense of who you are and what style works for you. Each one of us is a unique individual and we have a lot of different aspects to our personalities. Try creating your own self-inventory to figure out what you like and don't like. Self-awareness is a major key to feeling good, having the life you want, and not getting caught up in comparisons to other people. If you feel you've got a good handle on who you are, consider using this exercise as a moment of self-reflection and a "check-in" on how you're connecting with yourself.

1. **Write down at least 5 things that describe your personality.** Do this without judgment, as this is just part of the process of getting to know yourself.

2. **Write down at least 5 things that you would like other people to know about you.** Often, we feel that people don't "really know" us and there may be elements of yourself that you don't feel get expressed very often.

3. **Write down at least 5 things that you find helpful when you're anticipating meeting someone new** (this can be something about yourself (a fun fact is always a conversation-starter!), or something about a situation such as: talking face to face; entering an unknown situation with a friend; paying attention to how you dress for an occasion).

4. **Identify one thing about yourself that you don't like** or that you think interferes with your relationships. Create

a list of at least 5 things that you could do to address this issue.

5. **Write down at least 10 things that you like about yourself.** If you are having a hard time coming up with this list, consider asking close friends or family what they find positive or enjoyable about you.

6. **Take the Values In Action (VIA) Character survey** which can be found at https://www.viacharacter.org/. Try taking the longer version (both are free). Using the top 5 strengths identified in the VIA character survey, identify at least 2 areas where you demonstrate those strengths. Consider the whole 24-character strengths — what are at least 2 areas that you might like to improve or address? Write down at least 3 action steps you can do to take action.

7. **Take the 5 Love Languages quiz** which can be found at https://www.5lovelanguages.com/quizzes/. It gives you some insight into the kind of things that spell "love" to you (and what might matter to other people as well).

8. **Are substances (such as alcohol and cannabis) part of your life?** If so, take a moment to consider the circumstances in which you partake, the outcome, and any potential effect on your health or functioning.

See also: **Challenge 2:** Identifying Your Inner Voice
Challenge 3: Identifying Your Core Values
Challenge 5: Engaging in Self Care

Challenge 2.
Identifying Your Inner Voice

We all have an inner voice that "weighs in" on how we are living our life. For most of us, there are two main inner voices – one that is critical and focuses on the negative, and one that is more positive and nurturing. The inner critic tends to increase feelings of self-doubt, shame and blame, while your inner nurturer is kinder and more compassionate. It's also likely that your inner voice will change over time, as you encounter various life stages and milestones. Remember, this is not about judgment, it's about self-awareness.

1. **When you close your eyes and take a few deep breaths, what are the first thoughts or sensations that come to your awareness?** Write down what comes up. What does this tell you about what's going on with you?

2. **How often did you engage in negative self-talk over the last few days?** Negative self-talk is when you say things to yourself such as "I'm stupid" or "I will never get ahead." It takes practice to be able to recognize when this is happening.

3. **How often did you engage in positive, self-affirming talk over the past few days?** Positive, self-affirming talk involves saying things like, "I did a great job" or "I'm going to succeed." It takes practice to be able to recognize when this is happening as well.

4. **Consider keeping a record for a week of how often you are engaging in positive or negative self-talk.** This is going to give you a baseline of the frequency with which you

use both kinds of self-talk. Don't be surprised to find that the negative self-talk seems to increase once you are keeping track. This is completely normal. It's just pointing out that you haven't been noticing the degree to which those negative thoughts come up.

5. **Once you have a sense of how much you engage in positive and negative self-talk, you have succeeded at the first step of making a change — awareness.** It's pretty hard to change a behavior when you don't realize you're doing it! For the next week, each time that you notice an instance of negative self-talk, take a deep breath and ask yourself "what's the data to support this negative information?" Actively seek to counter the data with something positive. This will help you to begin to challenge and combat those negative thoughts — and it's strengthening the ability of your positive inner voice to be more nurturing and kinder.

6. **Imagine what you would say if someone you love talked about themselves using negative self-talk.** For the next week, after you challenge your negative thoughts, take your imagined response to your loved one and say it to yourself. This is allowing you to actively choose to engage in a more self-compassionate dialogue.

7. **Engage in the process of Awareness - Breath – Challenge – Compassion.** This means you first recognize that you're using negative self-talk, second take a deep breath, third challenge the negative statement, lastly say something compassionate to yourself. Over time, your negative self-talk will decrease!

See also: **Challenge 3:** Identifying Your Core Values

Challenge 4: When Fear is in Charge
(or Anxiety by Another Name)

Challenge 5: Engaging in Self-Care

Challenge 3.
Identifying Your Core Values

Your core values are the elements that shape your behavior, your decision-making, your choices, and the beliefs that you stand for. There's strong evidence that when we live in accordance with our values, we feel happier, more fulfilled, and are physically healthier. So how do you identify your values? Grab your notebook and pen, your phone or laptop and get ready to make some notes.

1. **Start by taking a deep breath and pretending this is like a mystery, where you will look for evidence and "clues" without any preconceived notions.** Recognize this is a lifelong process, and it's okay if you don't resolve it all right now.

2. **Already have some ideas about what might be values for you?** Go ahead and add them to your list.

3. **Glance at this list of 500 possible values, just to spark your thinking:** https://www.threadsculture.com/core-values-examples

4. **Begin a list identifying any issues that you have strong opinions about** — this can be anything from politics to the environment, to your views on monogamy.

5. **Think about the details of any experiences over your life that were really big or positive moments and add to your list from #2 what possible values you were demonstrating.** For example, your college graduation may be an indication of the value of perseverance or intellectual stimulation.

6. **Reviewing any difficult or challenging experiences in your life, add to your list any possible values you were demonstrating.**

7. **Review the positive and negative experiences again —** what values might you have missed or suppressed during these situations.

8. **Take another deep breath and clear your mind.** The goal isn't to delve into the emotions of your life, just to recognize the issues and ideals that make an impact on you.

9. **Consider situations in which you felt you "had" to make a certain decision based on your personal moral or ethical code.** What values did those situations represent? Add them to the list.

10. **What feels absolutely vital to have in your life?** Romance? Laughter? Money? No judgment, just add to your list the things/behaviors/concepts that are a "must have" for you.

11. **Think about the use of substances by partners and friends.** Is there a line that you don't want to cross or don't want your partner or friend to cross? What values does that line represent?

12. **Do you have strong political or religious beliefs that are vital to who you are?** If so, consider how this intersects with your values.

13. **Take a look at what you've come up with so far.** Try to identify the value present in each issue or experience. If you're having a hard time coming up with the descriptor, glance over the 500 values page again https://www.threadsculture.com/core-values-examples

14. **Here's where you will really drill down —** begin to group each of the values you've identified by theme/type — so

honesty, integrity, and telling the truth might be things you've identified that go into one group, while laughter, fun, and play make up a second group.

15. **Once you've defined your groups, pick a word that best represents the grouping.** It's likely to be one of the words you've identified, but it doesn't have to be.

16. **Chances are you will now have a list of 5-10 things that are vitally important to you, your happiness and your sense of purpose and fulfillment.** While some people suggest rank-ordering these, that's a personal choice. If it's on the list, it matters, and that's the goal.

See also: **Challenge 1:** Knowing What You Like

Challenge 2: Identifying Your Inner Voice

Challenge 8: Setting Realistic Goals and Crushing Them!

Challenge 4.
When Fear is in Charge
(or Anxiety by Another Name)

Fear is an unpleasant emotion caused by the belief that someone or something is dangerous, likely to cause pain, or a threat. It's one of the universal emotions across all human beings. The "threat" can be physical, emotional or psychological, and can be either a real or perceived danger. Fear is a vital part of our survival system, since fear is connected to our limbic system. The limbic system, led by the amygdala, generates the "flight/fight/freeze" response to help keep us safe. When the danger or threat is real, we want to have fear. We can also experience fear by imagining something that makes us afraid or uncomfortable, even if we know it's not real. Fear is the overall term for a range of emotions - from trepidation, nervousness, anxiety, dread, desperation, through to panic, horror, and terror. But the basic strategies to manage these emotions are the same, no matter what. (Side note — fear can also be a powerful tool and motivator, but that comes with allowing and recognizing the information that fear is sending, without getting caught up in letting fear be in charge).

1. **Create a list of the things (emotions, experiences, etc.) that bring up any level of fear for you,** then rank them from the lowest to highest level of fear.

2. **Get to know your physical signs of fear:** increased heart rate; feeling like you are going to vomit or that your heart is going to burst; muscle tension; stomachache; headache; difficulty sleeping or concentrating; shaking or trembling; feeling like you might faint. What do you experience when you're afraid?

3. **What are some of the thoughts or worries you have regarding fear?** This might include things like embarrassment, worried about rejection, looking foolish, drawing attention to yourself, not knowing what to say.

4. **Recognize the emotion.** Sometimes we mislabel fear as irritation, frustration or anger.

5. **Think about the ways in which fear has influenced your life.** Are there activities you would like to do, but don't? Friendships, relationships, jobs? Are there family experiences where you might be carrying someone else's fear?

6. **Identify a specific example that brings up fear for you.** What evidence do you have that the fear is real? Identify whether the fear is real, based in objective fact, (like working for a company that has announced they are having layoffs) or is a perceived fear (getting in trouble at work, even though you are a good, conscientious employee). Ask yourself this series of questions:

   a. What's the worst that can happen if this does come true?

   b. What's most likely to happen if it does come true?

   c. What will you do if it does come true?

   d. What are the chances that you will be ok?

7. **Imagine that tomorrow you woke up and all your fear was gone.** What would be different in your life? Write about this in your journal. Consider coming back later to review and add to your visualization.

8. **Identify a specific anxiety that you experience.** What evidence do you have that supports this anxiety being real? Identify whether the anxiety is based on objective fact, or is a perceived anxiety Ask yourself this series of questions:

   a. What's the worst that can happen if this does come true?

   b. What's most likely to happen if it does come true?

   c. What will you do if it does come true?

   d. What are the chances that you will be ok?

9. **Imagine that tomorrow you woke up and all your anxiety was gone.** What would be different in your life? Write about this in your journal. Consider coming back later to review and add to your visualization. In what ways was this similar or different from your imagined scenario about fear?

10. **Don't get caught in the "what ifs?"** It's easy to get stuck in an endless spiral of "what if" and that creates more fear/anxiety about a situation. Instead, think about the data — the identifiable facts about the situation — and what you can do in the present moment.

11. **Identify a good support person for you.** When you start taking charge of your fear, who can help you remember to breathe and go through the process of unpacking your fears?

See also: **Challenge 2:** Identifying Your Inner Voice

Challenge 6: When You Can't Say "No": Creating Healthy Boundaries

Challenge 7: When the Brave Front isn't Enough: How to Know when you Need Therapy

Challenge 5.
Engaging in Self-Care

Self-care is vital to managing your day-to-day life in the best possible manner. We all encounter stressors on an ongoing basis, and practicing self-care is how we reduce the negative effects of stress. Often people equate self-care with activities like a massage, bubble bath or making a purchase. These positive activities can be more of a "temporary fix" and are not a substitute for actual, ongoing self-care.

1. **The first component of self-care is the practice of self-compassion.** Self-compassion has 3 parts: mindfulness, self- kindness, and common humanity. Mindfulness involves being aware in the present moment without judgment. Self-kindness is treating yourself with the kindness you would show to a friend, or a loved one, instead of using negative, judgmental thoughts and behaviors. Common humanity is understanding that all human beings have the capacity for, and experience, the full range of human emotions.

2. **Make a commitment to yourself to practice self-compassion.** Do this by thinking of a time that you made a mistake or did something you felt was "wrong" and were upset with yourself. What happened? How did you react? What did you think and say to yourself? Consider what you would say to a close friend if they did the exact same thing you did. Say to yourself the same thing you would say to your friend. That's self-compassion. Repeat this process every time that you are thinking a negative thought about yourself.

3. **A toolbox of coping strategies is another element of self-care.** Positive coping strategies include things like talking to a friend, positive activities with your family, exercise, and doing something creative. What's in your toolbox?

4. **Identify any negative coping strategies you may be using,** such as eating, drinking, shopping, or using drugs when upset or stressed. Consider whether you want to reduce or eliminate the frequency with which you use those strategies.

5. **Set up an accountability partner for yourself** — someone who can (kindly) remind you when you are choosing negative coping strategies, or not using positive strategies.

6. **Self-awareness is a journey that takes practice.** Take 5 minutes each morning to meditate, do yoga, write in a journal or just have a cup of coffee and ponder. These 5 minutes are just for you to ask yourself two questions: "How do I want to feel today?" and "What do I need to happen today?"

7. **When you are working, take short breaks** (3-5 minutes) at least every 60-90 minutes. Use your break to stand and stretch, especially if you sit at a desk most of the day.

8. **Enjoy your meals.** Don't work while eating. Meet with co-workers/friends for meals, listen to podcasts, or enjoy the outdoors.

9. **Appreciate the view from your window** — or create a view if you don't have one by putting up pictures, posters or sayings that bring a smile to your face.

10. **Add plants to your workspace and your home.** Plants increase feelings of calm and warmth

11. **Use your vacation days and sick days.** Most people don't, and days off are a vital way to practice self-care!

See also: **Challenge 1:** Knowing What You Like

Challenge 2: Identifying Your Inner Voice

Challenge 7: When the Brave Front isn't Enough: How to Know when you Need Therapy

Challenge 6.
When You Can't Say "No":
Creating Healthy Boundaries

It's great to be helpful and willing to be involved. This can be a wonderful character strength and is often supported by a value system of service and altruism. On the other hand, the only way to effectively remain able to help and support others is by creating your own healthy boundaries. This involves a mixture of actions and attitude. If you or someone close to you is in a primary helping profession then ensuring healthy boundaries is especially important, as caregivers can be at particular risk of burnout through "over-giving" to others.

1. **Healthy boundaries** include assessing whether or not you are choosing to say "yes" based on interest/ability vs. obligation or perceived pressure (either implied or overt). Good boundaries also include being able to say "no" when something's not working for you — and being okay with that "no."

2. **Trying to please everyone is a surefire way to burn your boundaries,** and it is the antithesis of self-care. Start by recognizing when people-pleasing is your motivation.

3. **It's great to receive positive feedback or praise — but worrying about someone else's opinion can overshadow your own assessment.** Stop focusing on what others may think. You can't be everything to everyone, but you are responsible for being yourself.

4. **Stop apologizing and stop living in the past.** No matter how hard today may have been, a new day starts tomorrow.

If something's gone wrong, take responsibility, learn from it and apply it going forward.

5. **Embrace change as an opportunity to listen and trust your gut.** Just because something may not work the way you thought it would doesn't mean you should stop trying.

6. **Keep an eye on your schedule and make sure that you are carving out time for you.** Look for enough flexibility in your schedule so that you can include important and healthy activities such as exercise, time in nature and time with friends.

7. **You don't have to accept every invitation to dance —** which is the nice way of saying you are the person who is in charge of your decision-making. Compromise remains an important skill, but you'll manage stress (and multiple responsibilities) better when you're able to include "no" on a regular basis.

8. **Think about what your limits are, and then make it a practice to hold to them.** Instead of adding on "just one more thing", consider the option of letting go of one thing before taking on another.

9. **Think back to the values you defined in Challenge 3.** Are family, friends or partners engaging in behavior or beliefs that are contrary to your values?

10. **Be direct in communicating your limits and/or your concerns.** Dancing around the topic prolongs the agony, plus it increases the likelihood that you won't hold firm.

11. **Remember that relationships are interactions between people.** Having boundaries at work is similar to boundaries in our personal relationships, even though the circumstances are different.

12. **Give yourself permission** — permission to make the choices, decisions, actions and inactions that are consistent with your goals and values, not someone else's.

See also: **Challenge 4:** When Fear is in Charge (or Anxiety by Another Name)

                        Challenge 10: Having Healthy Conversations

                        Challenge 18: Agreeing to Disagree

Challenge 7.
When the Brave Front isn't Enough:
How to Know when you Need Therapy

As humans, we all encounter difficulties and challenges. This is literally how we learn and grow. When it comes to emotional issues, however, often we've developed a sense that we need to handle these situations "on our own", as if getting support is somehow a weakness. People also frequently fear that going to therapy is a sign that you're "crazy" (which is entirely untrue, and a completely outdated idea!). While therapy isn't necessary for every little bump in the road, particularly if you've got a good support system and self-care, there are also lots of reasons to consider going to therapy. Therapy is meant to be a safe, non-judgmental place to address your emotional concerns and develop the skills to handle various life challenges. Going to therapy is not a sign that you are "broken" — it's actually an action step towards feeling better!

1. **Here are some ways to know when it may be time to find a therapist:**

    a. You've been feeling sad, angry, or "not yourself" for more than a week or two.

    b. You're not performing as effectively at work or school as you previously did.

    c. You're sleeping or eating much more or much less than usual.

    d. You are struggling to build and maintain relationships (romantic or otherwise).

e. You're having problems with your physical health; you have a recent diagnosis related to your health or you're experiencing increased headaches, stomachaches or other physical pain (of course, check this out with your doctor first to rule out physical illness).

f. You are using alcohol, drugs, sex or food increasingly to cope with how you feel or what's going on in your life.

g. You've recently lost someone important to you — grief includes loss of important relationships to circumstances as well as to death. The end of a long-term friendship, mentorship or romantic relationship can be really difficult.

h. You've experienced a traumatic event or are having lots of memories or reactions to trauma in your past.

i. You've stopped do the activities you typically enjoy or feel an overall lack of interest.

j. You're having difficulty regulating your emotions (sadness, anger, anxiety).

k. You find yourself withdrawing from friends and/or family.

l. You want to make changes in your life but don't know where to start.

m. You're having difficulty setting healthy boundaries.

n. You're in a transition phase (such as changing your job/career, moving, etc.).

o. Someone who cares about you has compassionately suggested that you go to therapy.

2. **To find a therapist, you can ask your primary care doctor (if you have one) for recommendations.** You can ask someone you trust for recommendations or look online for therapists in your area — https://www.psychologytoday.com/us is a great resource.

3. **Check your insurance.** Your insurance company can give you a list of covered providers.

4. **Consider a few sessions to start:** Many employers offer a few free sessions of therapy through Employee Assistance Programs (EAP).

5. **After you identify a potential therapist, do a quick interview to see if you feel comfortable or have a connection.** It's totally ok to decide to not work with someone if it doesn't feel right. Most therapists will have a quick, no-cost phone conversation with you before you decide to work together.

6. **If you start therapy and feel like you're not making progress, like you're not being heard or understood, or if you just don't like the vibe, talk to your therapist to see if this can change.** If it doesn't — you don't have to stay with this therapist!

7. **Keep in mind that therapy doesn't have to last for a lifetime.** It's an opportunity to get support and guidance on addressing issues and building skills. Lots of people attend fewer than 8 sessions. At the same time, don't give up after a couple of sessions; sometimes it can take a while to work through things. There's no "right" or "wrong" — it's about what's right for you.

See also: **Challenge 4:** When Fear is in Charge (or Anxiety by Another Name)

Challenge 5: Engaging in Self-Care

Challenge 31: After the Breakup

Challenge 8.
Setting Realistic Goals and Crushing Them!

You have lots of ideas of what you'd like to accomplish, but somehow, you still fall behind. First of all, realize that you're not alone. Goal setting is a skill — and it's not one we tend to teach in school! Many times, people get caught up striving for perfection, and this keeps them stuck. There's a phrase "procrastination by perfection". It's important to remember that the point is to meet your goals, not have them be "perfect".

1. **Set goals that you actually want to achieve.** This is vital, since we let our goal setting often be determined by "shoulds", rather than "wants" or "needs."

2. **Goals aligned with your core values are easier to stick with.** It's also helpful to articulate the "why" behind your goal so when it gets hard you can remind yourself.

3. **Identify the overall content areas that you wish to address.** This could include career; finance; education; relationship; physical/health; emotional/mental health; attitude/perspective.

4. **Brainstorm what feels important to you,** differentiating this from any "shoulds" or external expectations.

5. **Write down a list of the major areas,** from most important or pressing, to least.

6. **Now break down your list into component,** or sub-goals. For example, if you want to go back to school, sub-goals might include looking for available programs; determining the admission criteria; assessing financial aid; deter-

mining a plan for time management, etc. There are likely many more steps, and these sub-goals often can be broken down even further.

7. **Follow the SMART process to define your goals**. Ensure your goals are:

     a. S – Specific

     b. M – Measurable

     c. A – Action-Oriented

     d. R – Rewarding

     e. T – Trackable (regarding time and progress)

8. **Pick ONE goal to start working on.** Too often people try to address multiple goals at the same time, which takes longer, and dilutes the process. Write down your goal, in SMART format and put it in several visible and accessible places (bathroom mirror, door of the fridge, inside of your planner).

9. **Estimate the time needed to reach each step of your goal.** If you're not sure, ask someone with experience in that area for their opinion.

10. **Plan and schedule time in your day to address your goal.** Don't wait until you're "in the mood" (that's one of the main reason people fall off in progress). Start with small goals and short time frames. Using the example above, you might schedule (2) 15-minute times during the week when you will research doctoral programs.

11. **State each goal as a positive statement** (what you will do, not what you "won't" do).

12. **Have a contingency plan.** There's a great phrase "no plan survives first contact" which means that it's important to

recognize the ways in which problems may arise and have a general outline on an alternative so you can adapt and keep moving forward.

13. **If you achieved the goal really easily,** make your next goal a little harder. Similarly, if it took a long time to meet your goal, make sure your next goal a little easier or break your goals into smaller steps — you are working to build on success.

14. **If a goal is too big then it can seem like you're not making progress.** If this happens, clarify your sub-goals that will help you reach your big goal. Keeping these sub-goals small and incremental gives you greater rewards.

15. **Create a daily "to-do" list — and keep it manageable!** Overcommitting is another procrastination trap.

16. **Believe in the process** — imagine that each one of the steps towards your goal is a Lego block. It takes a lot of tiny blocks to make a structure.

17. **Identify and celebrate the small steps** you made in the right direction even if you didn't reach the final goal.

18. **If you run into an obstacle,** ask your support system for help in identifying a solution or offering a different perspective.

19. **Keep in mind that if you do not reach your goal this does not make you a failure.** It's a process, so analyze which of the SMART steps needs adjustment. Ask yourself what you learned from the experience that might help you in achieving future goals. Adapting your expectations and priorities is part of the growth process. While we may not achieve every goal exactly as we imagined, we always have the opportunity to learn and move forward, even if it's in a new direction.

20. **Celebrate your achievements and be proud of your accomplishments!**

See also: **Challenge 1:** Knowing What You Like

Challenge 3: Identifying Your Core Values

Challenge 5: Engaging in Self-Care

Challenge 9.
The Dark Side of Social Media: It's Not About the "Likes"

Social media has become a part of almost everyone's life. Although the platforms may differ (even some of the holdouts are leaving Facebook, and Instagram is upping its video game with "Reels" to pick up the slack from Tik-Tok), it's rare to find a Millennial who doesn't have some social media presence. Many people get their news from social media such as Twitter or Facebook. Snapchat and Instagram remain consistently high-use platforms. While there are a lot of benefits to social media (easy communication, connection, new ideas, etc.), there's also a lot of potential negative effects that are worth keeping in mind as you determine the best social media practices for yourself.

1. **Social media can be problematic.** There is a connection between posting selfies and self-absorption; if your use of selfies and filters prevents you from enjoying the moment you're in, it's not working in your best interest. Spending a lot of time on social media may result in overspending, which can have a negative effect on your financial well-being. It's also true that spending increased time looking at pictures of delicious food can result in neuro-physical changes in your brain that lead to increased feelings of hunger over time. Social media often leaves users vulnerable to cyberbullying and hate speech.

2. **Blue light (from your device) disrupts sleep patterns,** so social media use at night (especially in bed) can interfere with getting a good night's sleep. Need your nighttime fix? Consider getting blue light glasses as a first step.

3. **Comparing yourself and your life to what others post on social media frequently leads to a sense of inadequacy about your life or appearance.** For example, social media star Rachel Hollis developed a platform of "transparency" but didn't disclose her marital troubles for over a year. You don't always know what's going on with social media, so take their "perfect" lives with a big grain of salt.

4. **Your self-esteem can be impacted when you post something you feel is important or memorable, and you don't get the amount of "likes" that you might expect.** Even though you get a dopamine hit with likes, when you're anticipating a big response and it doesn't come, that's not a reflection of your worth.

5. **A lot of social media is based upon an algorithm.** So, you could have the next Tik Tok dance or cutest viral cat video but if it's not within the algorithm then no one will see it. We didn't like algorithms in math class so don't use it to compare your life.

6. **Consider comparing social media "likes" with the true opinions of people you value in your life.** Decide that the opinion of a trusted few is more important than the "poll results" on social media.

7. **FOMO (Fear of missing out) is a real struggle for many people**, especially when it appears that others are doing more fun or exciting things. Your life is the one you are living. Find the things that are fun and engaging for you, and do them, staying in the moment.

8. **Using social media as your main tool of connection, rather than in-person or virtual face-to-face interactions can lead to a sense of isolation,** especially when combined with comparison and FOMO. Don't forget to maintain your real, in-person relationships.

9. **Your social media consumption may be leading to unrealistic expectations** regarding success, achievements or even the degree of romance in your relationship. Remember to value what you have and work towards the goals that actually matter to you.

10. **Getting a like or a reply on social media tends to activate your brain's reward system,** which can lead to increased use of social media, establishing a pattern that's similar to addiction.

See also:

Challenge 2: Identifying Your Inner Voice

Challenge 5: Engaging in Self-Care

Challenge 37: Navigating Social Media: Ego and Etiquette

Challenge 10.
Having Healthy Conversations

One of the primary ways we get to know other people and develop relationships, as well as learn about ourselves, is through conversation. Although it's important to know your values and your boundaries, it's also important to know what to discuss and when. Timing and word choice can make or break a conversation, as well as a relationship – and this is true at work, with friends, partners and family.

1. **Recognize the setting and any potential "norms" that may be involved.** For example, many organizations frown on swearing or discussions of politics or religion in the workplace. Know the limits of what is considered acceptable and watch your language.

2. **Pay attention to what the other person is saying.** (This is also known as "listening.") If you're concentrating on your response, you're likely to miss important subtleties in their language — as well as the content!

3. **Begin from a place of curiosity and respect,** and don't worry about being liked.

4. **Expect a positive outcome,** even if you are discussing a difficult topic.

5. **Speak directly to the other person and give them your full attention.** Conversing with a real-life person is not a time to be on your phone, Snapchatting or posting on Instagram.

6. **Stay calm**. This increases the chance that others will hear what you're saying, rather than responding to your emotions. Don't be afraid to ask for a time-out if you are unable to stay calm in the moment.

7. **Be empathic.** If the other person is getting heated or showing increased emotion, do your best to understand where they are coming from and what's driving their reaction. Work to kindly help the conversation forward.

8. **Allow give and take in the conversation.** This includes pausing to ask the other person questions and listening to the other person to ask questions. Do your best to respond honestly, and then pass the ball back to them.

9. **Avoid blaming or literally pointing your finger** — this increases reactivity and decreases positive communication.

10. **Treat the other person with respect.**

11. **No interrupting**.

12. **Drop your assumptions** and be open to learning and understanding, rather than jumping to conclusions.

13. **If the conversation brings up feelings for you,** take responsibility for your own feelings — no one can make you feel a certain way. It's also important to remember that your feelings are valid and you have a right to voice them.

See also: **Challenge 2:** Identifying Your Inner Voice

Challenge 6: When You Can't Say "No": Creating Healthy Boundaries

Challenge 18: Agreeing to Disagree

Challenge 25: Fighting "Fair"

Challenge 11.
Being Labeled a "Millennial"

You know who you are — and it's more than a one-word stereotype. Technically, Millennials are the people born between about 1980 and 2000. This means that right now as a group, some millennials are around 40 years old, but the youngest are just hitting 20. There's a lot of possible life difference between 20 years and 40 years old. Just like any other label, being called a Millennial may seem a perfect fit, or you may not think it applies to you at all.

1. **Only 40% of Millennials actually identify as Millennials** according to the Pew Research Center. Labels are easy to use, but ultimately, it's up to you whether it's something you identify with or not.

2. **Descriptions of Millennials in the media tend to be negative** — "self-absorbed", "wasteful", "greedy" — and these are the characterizations made by Millennials! Baby Boomers and Generation X have said lots of negative things about Millennials, but this doesn't mean it's true about the entire generation or true about you specifically. Every generation says negative things about younger generations. It's not personal, and not even necessarily accurate! Plus, there are many good things about Millennials too.

3. **Given the dramatic age differences** between ends of the Millennial spectrum, it can be hard to identify the whole group, especially if you're on the older or younger edges of the group.

4. **There are many positive stereotypes of Millennials!** Wanting to travel, take care of the environment, and enter into marriage/commitment later than previous generations are signs of self-reliance, inspiration and compassion. Millennials are generally quite media-savvy, open to change, and resilient. Millennials are also the best educated generation and often willing to try new things and take risks.

5. **If someone calls you a Millennial,** it doesn't affect who you are — even if you don't like the label. The label doesn't make you more likely to enjoy avocado toast or post selfies just like it doesn't reflect your level of productivity or work ethic. Take it in stride and keep going!

See also: **Challenge 2:** Identifying Your Inner Voice

Challenge 9: The Dark Side of Social Media: It's Not About the "Likes"

Challenge 37: Navigating Social Media: Ego and Etiquette

Part 2.
Relationship with Peers

Challenge 12.
Making Friends as a Grown-up

Once you've finished with high school or college, it can feel almost impossible to meet new people and make new friends. This is especially true if you've moved to a new area where you don't have any connections (or if everyone around you is starting a family and no one has time to hang out!). Here are some ways to meet people — and remember, you've got to be willing to step outside your comfort zone a little!

1. **One of the easiest ways to meet someone is through your existing friends.** Consider asking to be included when a friend is getting together with a bunch of people.

2. **Work is an excellent place to meet friends** and is often the most common way people expand their social circle. Keep in mind that friendships with your supervisor or someone you supervise can bring additional challenges.

3. **Think about the activities that interest you** (or that you've considered but never done) and take a class or join a group. Consider cooking, writing, yoga, or running, and then talk to other people who are attending.

4. **Book clubs are a great way to meet people,** and even in the time of COVID-19 are an accessible way to increase your circle. Find a book club that meets your interests — social justice, mysteries, women's fiction — and then sign up.

5. **The Meetup app has a wide variety of activities.** Consider trying something you wouldn't normally do!

6. **Using a co-working space is another way to meet people and get work done.** Consider doing your work at a local coffee shop and talk to the baristas or other regulars.

7. **Join a sports team.** Now that everyone's an adult, there's often a big social aspect, including going out for lunch, dinner or beers after games.

8. **If you have a dog, the dog park is a great option** — exercise your dog and meet other dog owners.

9. **Following someone interesting on Instagram or LinkedIn?** Reply to their posts, engage with their content and start a conversation.

10. **Travel** — whether it's across the country or across the world is a great way to expand your friendships – once it's post-pandemic safe.

11. **Check out local options for volunteering.** This is an opportunity to help others while meeting new people.

12. **Get to know your neighbors.** Suggest a pot-luck dinner as a way to get together.

13. **Joining a wine or beer tasting tour** is a fun way to meet new people.

14. **Consider going to church, temple, or another faith-based organization.**

15. **If there's a speaking club in your area such as Toastmasters,** you can improve your confidence in public speaking and make connections.

16. **Networking events and conferences** provide groups of new people and connections.

17. **Apps aren't just for dating** — some people use them to meet friends. Be clear about your boundaries and what you're looking for.

18. **Make a commitment to accepting invitations** (even when you're not in the mood) and to take the initiative to start conversations.

See also: **Challenge 2:** Identifying Your Inner Voice

Challenge 13: Reading Vibes Quickly

Challenge 14: Friendship Dealbreakers

Challenge 13.
Reading Vibes Quickly

Meeting new people has the potential to be really beneficial, but there can also be a downside. You might really feel the groove, start hanging out and then — bam! — it all goes wrong. Pay attention to the vibes from the beginning to figure out if this is a go or a no-go connection.

1. **Body language is your secret weapon to understanding the meaning behind the words.** This goes for what you're putting out as well as what you're reading from others.

2. **Whether we like it or not, appearance makes a difference.** If you're totally turned off by the slogan on their t-shirt, take a pass. Same goes for issues of cleanliness — if your standards are at odds from the beginning, you're not likely to get over that soon.

3. **Posture** tells you whether someone is potentially too aggressive (taking up all the space), defensive (folded in on themselves) or just not interested (turned away and avoiding eye contact).

4. **Pay attention to their facial expressions.** We often aren't aware of all the micro-expressions that cross our face, but they're more visible to others.

5. **What's their physical movement like?** Are they taking up too much space or do you feel uncomfortable by their frequent touching or large body moments?

6. **If they've shaken your hand or hugged you, notice how you feel.** If you want to wipe your hand off or back away,

this is a big red flag. Don't forget — it's also totally cool to say no to a hug. You are in charge of your own boundaries and comfort level!

7. **Whether or not the eyes are the "window to the soul", there's a lot to learn.** If they avoid eye contact, or their smile doesn't crinkle their eyes, there's a good chance they're not fully into you. This can also suggest some discomfort with intimacy. It may not be a dealbreaker, but it's worth paying attention to.

8. **Are they checking out other people while you're together or seeing who else is in the room?** Even for friends, this is a sign of disengagement in the moment.

9. **Notice how you feel about their tone of voice.** Do they sound overly critical or negative, or super sweet and insincere? This includes how they respond to other people — you want your relationships (friends and otherwise) to be authentic and genuine.

10. **Listen with curiosity.** Sometimes it takes people a while to relax and open up, so unless all the alarms are going off, allow a little time to assess.

11. **Pay attention to expressions of empathy.** We all want to be treated well and understood, and empathy is vital for this.

12. **What is your gut instinct telling you?** If your mind says, "They're great", but your gut says something is off — pay attention!

13. **Notice how you feel.** Flattery and validation feel good but check for feelings of substance. If you feel enriched by the interaction, that's a great sign.

See also: **Challenge 12:** Making Friends as a Grown-up

Challenge 14: Friendship Dealbreakers

Challenge 19: Knowing What You're Looking For

Challenge 14.
Friendship Dealbreakers

We have a variety of friendships throughout our life, and not all friendships last forever. This is totally cool, as sometimes people simply grow in different directions. Friendships are meant to be a two-way street, where you each contribute to maintaining and strengthening the relationship. Note, this is not the same as keeping score. As two different individuals, you bring specific strengths (and weaknesses) to the relationship. While it's healthy for there to be give and take, make sure it's not ALWAYS you who is the one giving, or the one always taking — everyone has hard times where they need more support — but ultimately the relationship should be fairly balanced. Still, sometimes you have to end a friendship that isn't working for you. This is an incomplete list of friendship dealbreakers; ultimately you have to make that choice for yourself.

1. **A relationship that is completely one-sided**, where you are doing all the initiating or accommodating or putting in all the effort to keep it going and keep in contact, isn't good for either of you.

2. **Feeling like you have to spotlessly clean the house before your friend comes over** may be a sign you're concerned about impressing them. This could also be a sign you don't feel confident in who you are.

3. **If they offer unsolicited advice about parenting, dating, work** — pretty much any topic where you're not asking for feedback but they feel you "need to know." Especially if they keep pressuring you to take their advice.

4. **If you're the backup friend when no one else is available,** that's a dealbreaker.

5. **If your friend has no sense of humor,** or a completely different (unrelatable) sense of humor, especially if it's around making fun of or putting down other people.

6. **Friend can't keep a secret?** Loves to gossip about others? You're heading for hurt, because sooner or later, you'll be the subject of their gossip.

7. **They won't introduce you to their friends,** but are happy to hang out with you and your friends. It's concerning when people won't introduce you to their people.

8. **Cancelling plans without warning on a regular basis** (which is also a sign of being a "back-up friend").

9. **They compete with you** or they try to make you jealous (similar to competing for you, this is a total no-go).

10. **They need constant attention** but there's no consideration of you or your needs or interests.

11. **They put you down, pick fights with you, or lack empathy.**

12. **They are regularly judgmental** — of you, your friends or your values.

13. **They're not present when you're together,** such as they are always on the phone.

14. **They create drama (no one needs that!).**

15. **You feel exhausted by the idea of hanging out.**

16. **You can't be yourself.**

17. **They are consistently pushing you** to do things too far outside your comfort zone or that are against your values.

18. **Repeatedly guilting you into doing whatever they want to do** and not taking into account your wants or needs

19. **Lack of boundaries around emotional issues** — dumping all their emotions and problems on you without asking permission/expressing gratitude and not being there to listen to you reciprocally

See also: **Challenge 13:** Reading Vibes Quickly

Challenge 16: Breaking up with a Friend – or when a Friend Breaks up with You

Challenge 18: Agreeing to Disagree

Challenge 15.
Colleagues, Friends or Both?

It's no surprise that when people spend a lot of time together at work, friendships begin to develop. Over the course of a work week, we often spend more time with our colleagues than anyone else. It's possible to have work relationships develop into a solid friendship, but you will do best to consider the possible risks and benefits.

1. **Developing a strong rapport with a colleague** can help you know each other better and can build greater interest, compassion, and respect. Work can be a lot more fun and enjoyable because you're able to be yourself. Mutual respect and connection may allow you to be more engaged and committed to supporting each other.

2. **Always be considerate of their lifestyle and needs.** A new parent doesn't have the same free time as the happily single co-worker.

3. **Don't rush the relationship.** Sharing your deepest secrets with a colleague can put you both in an uncomfortable position if they're not on the same page.

4. **You both need to be emotionally mature and responsible** for this to work. Transparency and honesty are key to allowing a work relationship to develop into a workable, mutual friendship.

5. **Consider how close you are (or want to be) to your boss or subordinates.** Is it about shared values or interests, or a form of favoritism?

6. **Both parties need to be on board with respecting boundaries** and be able to say "no" if something doesn't feel right.

7. **Be aware of any power dynamics that might be at play** and be willing to address them honestly. This is especially true in boss/subordinate relationships.

8. **Disagreements and differences of opinion are common in friendships and at work.** You both need to be able to manage your feelings and emotions when this comes up.

9. **If you're spending all your time talking about work issues,** you may be connecting but it's not a friendship, it's a vent session — know the difference.

10. **Be prepared for what to do if things go sideways.** You don't want your thoughts and feelings about a friendship gone bad to impact your work.

11. **Getting drunk or high with co-workers has an impact on how others see you,** so be cautious.

12. **Don't feel bad if you don't want to socialize with co-workers** — you don't have to be best friends with everyone. If you're sure you want to separate work and personal life, consider attending out of work events for a short time to maintain connections. You can be "friends" at different levels of closeness/intimacy.

13. **Allow yourself the option of developing a relationship or not,** considering all of the factors. No situation is exactly the same, so stay tuned-in to your values.

See also: **Challenge 6:** When You Can't Say "No": Creating Healthy Boundaries

Challenge 13: Reading Vibes Quickly

Challenge 18: Agreeing to Disagree

Challenge 16.
Breaking up with a Friend – or When a Friend Breaks up with You

You've been besties forever — or at least it feels that way — but recently things just aren't clicking. Maybe you've encountered some of the Friendship Dealbreakers (see Challenge 14) or you've just decided it's not working for you. Or perhaps your friend is ending it with you. Whatever the situation, here are some important things to remember.

1. **If you're figuring out what to do,** it's okay to have a little distance by decreasing contact to give you some space to assess the situation.

2. **Decide whether this is a friendship you want to repair or end.** Sometimes it's not possible to repair a situation, but it helps to know your preference.

3. **Consider talking through the situation with a trusted confidant.** This doesn't mean trashing your friend to your other bestie. Finding a neutral person (and maybe not naming the friend) may allow for more objectivity.

4. **Be clear about your goals.** Journaling, writing a letter that you do not have to send might help you identify what you want if the friendship goes forward.

5. **Be honest with yourself,** and plan to be honest when dealing with your friend.

6. **Treat your friend with respect.** You've had a connection, so honor the relationship. This means no ghosting.

7. **Keep your sense of compassion at the forefront.** Whatever's gone on, you'll feel better by recognizing that we all face difficulties in life.

8. **Don't engage in drama.** Getting all worked up won't help anyone.

9. **Plan to talk to your friend in person, not through text or email.** There's a lot of room for misunderstanding when it's all through text, so give your friendship the benefit of a face-to-face talk.

10. **Start with what's been good about the friendship.** Share some of the things that you like about them and drew you together.

11. **Use "I" statements which will help you avoid being defensive, aggressive or accusatory.** Address your concerns by using something like "I've been bothered by....", or ".... Doesn't feel good to me". Don't say things like "You always..." or "You never....".

12. **Do your best to stay away from blame,** even if you totally feel you're justified and in the right.

13. **Keep in mind that a friendship ending doesn't mean that either of you are a bad person.** It's just means that you're not as compatible as you once thought.

14. **It's likely that you will feel a sense of loss.** For some people, the end of a close friendship is more painful than a romantic breakup, especially if it's a longstanding relationship.

15. **Get support from others who have gone through similar issues** — but this does not mean gossiping to your other friends.

16. **If you're on the receiving end of the friendship break-up,** remember it's ok for you to ask for an explanation (even if they choose to not give one to you).

17. **If there's been actual abuse in the relationship,** you certainly don't need to meet in person (safety first always!), and this might be the time for a phone call or email that simply asks the person not to contact you again.

See also: **Challenge 6:** When You Can't Say "No": Creating Healthy Boundaries

Challenge 14: Friendship Dealbreakers

Challenge 18: Agree to Disagree

Challenge 17.
Buds to Boo: Benefits and Risks

You've got your go-to friend, the one who's always there when you have a break-up, or a problem at work. You've both dated other people, and don't let those other relationships come between your friendship. And then something happens. You start looking them a little differently — maybe wondering why you never noticed how attractive you find them. Or maybe you're picking up on a new vibe from them and wondering what to do.

1. **Before jumping in with a declaration of love or lust, ask yourself what you are really feeling.** Is this something that's been building, or is this a reaction to some recent event or interaction? Give yourself a little time to determine if this is more than just a momentary thought.

2. **Recognize that making the transition from friends to something more can be awkward** — even more so if this is a one-sided situation. Consider what's potentially at stake. If they aren't into you, will they still be your friend? Will you want them to? Think about whether you're willing to lose the friendship if things don't work out.

3. **Figure out what you want from them** — are you thinking booty call, friend with benefits, or serious relationship? If you're connected because you're so different that it's a great break from your everyday life, that might suggest a friend with benefits or booty call situation. If you're thinking their values and life plans are in accord with yours, that might suggest a serious relationship.

4. **Keep in mind that the qualities we find attractive about someone are often what is also most repelling.** For

example, a friend who always makes you laugh can seem like they don't take life seriously when things get stressful.

5. **On the plus side, you are working with a relationship that is based in trust and already has a solid base.** You already know a lot about them. Those late-night talks over ice-cream or drinks when things have gone wrong gives you a lot of information about their capacity for support, compassion and understanding. You also have some shared social networks, so integrating into their friend group won't be hard (although there's always the possibility that it might be a little awkward at first).

6. **If you do want to talk about changing your friendship, wait until neither of you is in a romantic relationship.** If you're the one recognizing feelings for your friend, get out of any current relationship you're in first.

7. **You've already practiced being open and honest about lots of feelings, so if you're ready to have "the talk"** about these feelings, keep being clear and upfront. Be honest with yourself (and your new boo) about what is and isn't working.

8. **A deep friendship is the strongest base for a romantic relationship,** so if you're falling for your best friend, you've already got a positive start.

See also: **Challenge 1:** Knowing What You Like

Challenge 13: Reading Vibes Quickly

Challenge 17: Knowing What You're Looking For

Challenge 18.
Agreeing to Disagree

None of us are always on the same page all the time. Even the closest of friends sometimes see things very differently, and that's ok. You might already know the hot buttons in your friendship, or you might be caught off guard by a sudden difference of opinion. There's a process you can follow that preserves the friendship and lets you get to agreeing to disagree.

1. **If you want to address a situation where you disagree,** take a few moments to prepare your thoughts. You can address the disagreement in the moment by saying something like, "Wait a minute... I have a different perspective on that." Or you can return to the conversation later, like "Hey, when you talked about xxx before, it raised some questions for me..."

2. **If it's about something that's important to you, don't put off the conversation until "someday."** Avoiding the topic can create an underlying rift in the friendship.

3. **Expect a positive outcome.** Even if you don't end up seeing eye to eye on everything, that doesn't necessarily mean the relationship has to end. Of course, there are limits. If your friend disagrees on a topic that you are passionate about, or which is a dealbreaker for you, consider whether you want to maintain the friendship.

4. **Approach the conversation with an interest in problem solving or finding common ground,** rather than needing to be "right." If you need to be "right" it means the other person has to be "wrong." That's not a sign of a continuing

friendship. Make certain you are coming from a place of empathy and curiosity. Don't blame your friend or decide you know what they think before you've had the conversation.

5. **Be specific and direct** about the topic you want to discuss.

6. **Maintain respect.** This is your friend, so treat them like it. No name-calling or put-downs. No interrupting. And stay at the same eye level, so neither one of you is forced to look up or down.

7. **Don't expend your energy worrying about being liked.** Your belief in a positive outcome, compassion, curiosity and respect will help you navigate the situation.

8. **Pay attention to your language.** This means staying away from extremes (like "always" or never") and not assuming you know their reasoning.

9. **No finger-pointing**, either figuratively, by verbally blaming or literally, by actually pointing your finger at them.

10. **Manage your emotional response.** Speak as calmly as possible. Getting upset and/or agitated decreases effective conversation. Don't respond until you understand what they are saying. If you're not sure what they mean, ask for clarification.

11. **Allow time for your friend to ask questions** or consider their response.

12. **When describing your concerns/questions or what you'd like to happen differently,** be as clear as possible and use specific examples.

13. **Keep to the topic you're discussing.** Don't bring up a laundry list of everything you've ever disagreed with them about.

14. **Don't make it personal or take it personally.** Your goal is understanding, as well as maintaining the relationship.

15. **Don't just walk away or opt out of the conversation.** If it's starting to become heated, consider taking a time-out to give everyone the chance to calm down and compose themselves.

16. **Take responsibility for your own feelings.** This means knowing what's coming up for you emotionally.

17. **If you've both expressed your thoughts and opinions and you still disagree,** try thanking them for being willing to talk about this with you.

18. **Appreciate the qualities of the relationship you admire** and remember that differences don't mean the person is "bad".

19. **Fundamental differences in values** may involve friendship dealbreakers (see **Challenge #14**) or even a friendship break up (see **Challenge #16**). Although this can be difficult, it's always ok to stick to your personal values and beliefs.

See also:

Challenge 14: Friendship Dealbreakers

Challenge 16: Breaking Up with a Friend – or When a Friend Breaks Up with You

Challenge 20: Finding "The One"

Part 3.
Relationship with Romantic Partners

Challenge 19.
Knowing What You're Looking For

You've decided you're ready to have a romantic partner, but you're not sure what exactly you want. Maybe you've had prior relationships that didn't go well, or you can't remember the last time you had a romantic relationship. Either way, it's a great opportunity to figure out what it is you're looking for in a partner.

1. **Create a list of all the possible desirable traits** you'd like to see in a partner. Be creative and come back to the list a few times to see what you can add.

2. **Look at the bad dates or relationships you had** — this is a way to identify what you *don't* want in a relationship.

3. **Think about what went well (and badly) in prior relationships.** What characteristics did the person have? What made this a good relationship?

4. **Consider how you want to feel in a relationship.** Imagine you are with someone — what are the feelings that you want to experience as part of a relationship?

5. **Go back to knowing yourself (*Challenge 1: Knowing What You Like*)** and see if there's anything else to add to your potential partner list.

6. **Review (or do!) the work from *Challenge 3: Identifying Your Core Values*.** Values are important drivers for knowing and having what you want.

7. **Start journaling about a relationship** and be super honest with yourself.

8. **Think about your sexuality.** Allow yourself to do a self-inventory around what you are attracted to or might consider.

9. **Create a vision board that reflects what you want in a romantic partner.** This is a great way to get at some of your subconscious thoughts and feelings. Grab a bunch of magazines (or pictures from the internet) that intrigue you or capture your interest and make a collage. See what qualities jump out after you do this.

10. **Take a few deep breaths and let yourself feel open, honest and vulnerable.** Ask yourself "what do I need in a relationship?" and notice what comes up for you.

11. **Identify your non-negotiables.** You might get some ideas from *Challenge 14: Friendship Dealbreakers*. If you won't tolerate it in a friendship, it's not a great basis for a romantic relationship.

12. **Identify any red flags** that might be related to your non-negotiables. Red flags are early warning signs that the person may be heading towards a non-negotiable (such as openly flirting or getting other people's numbers, when monogamy is a non-negotiable for you).

13. **Talk to other people who are in healthy relationships about what works and what doesn't,** as well as what they've learned about red flags. You don't have to incorporate all (or any!) of what they share, but it gives you a place to start.

14. **Take a look at *Challenge 6: When you can't say "No!"*** Creating healthy boundaries will help you pay attention to your needs and limits.

15. **Think about your childhood, and the positives and negatives in relationships that you experienced or observed** growing up. This may give some additional clarity to knowing what you want (and what you don't).

16. **Consider what you might tell a friend about identifying important qualities in a relationship.** This can give you some hidden insight into what matters to you.

17. **Look at your list and assess how many traits and characteristics are an actual reflection of you.** This is an opportunity to move from "wish list" to "what really matters" and gives you a chance to make sure your expectations are reasonable.

18. **Use your journal to imagine what you want after the "honeymoon" stage.** Even if it's all hearts and flowers in the beginning, lasting relationships generally settle into a more moderate lifestyle.

19. **Make sure that you're making time for yourself,** both in the present and in your future romance. This will help you stay on-track with what you want.

See also: **Challenge 1:** Knowing What You Like

Challenge 3: Identifying Your Core Values

Challenge 6: When You Can't Say "No": Creating Healthy Boundaries

Challenge 14: Friendship Dealbreakers

Challenge 20.
Finding "The One"

Now that you've spent some time thinking about the kind of relationship you want, it's time to put your ideas into action with a real person. You're in the dating world and wondering "Is this the one?" Here's some of the things you'll want to consider.

1. **Emotional maturity.** Everyone has some flaws and emotional baggage, but we each need to carry our own. Making sure you're at equivalent emotional stages is important.

2. **Do the two of you have the same values and life plans?** If you're thinking house and kids and they are wanting solo travel, this may not be a great match.

3. **Are you both looking for the same kind of relationship?** When they want a fling and you're looking for forever, it's not the right relationship.

4. **Pay attention to how you feel about yourself when you're with them.** If you feel better about yourself, that's awesome. If you're trying to please or impress, that's a big no.

5. **Openness, honesty and respect are vital** no matter what kind of relationship you're looking for, and if it's not there, it's not "the one".

6. **Independence and the appreciation of some "alone time" are important.** You don't need to be joined at the hip 24/7, and healthy relationships work best when you have both overlapping and separate interests.

7. **Pay attention to the degree and type of physical affection that you are looking for vs. what you're getting.** Major differences in this area can be cause for later dissatisfaction.

8. **If you're having sex, make sure it's working for both of you.** This includes frequency, intensity, duration and type. Going out of your comfort zone is ok, but you don't want to feel pressured, uncomfortable or uneasy.

9. **Having a similar sense of humor.** The ability to make each other laugh and having fun together is a wonderful counterbalance to the stressors that come up in life.

10. **Do they have friends?** How does it go when they're with their friends (or the two of you are with your friends)? Do you like their friends? Do they get along with your friends?

11. **Are they willing to work through disagreements and challenges?** Do they fight fairly or is every disagreement a big blow up? Check in with Challenge 10: Having Healthy Conversations and Challenge 18: Agreeing to Disagree for some pointers on this.

12. **Ask yourself if they are empathic and kind.** This is connected to emotional support and validation, which we all need at times. It's long been said that how people treat waitstaff and other servers says a lot about their personality.

13. **Pay attention to the ways they express or look for emotional intimacy and think about your own needs for intimacy.** There's always room for growth and learning about each other, but a lack of perceived intimacy hurts a relationship.

14. **Slow down and give yourself time!** Lasting, healthy relationships don't magically develop overnight. Those early pheromones may make it seem perfect but give yourself (and the relationship) a chance to grow before deciding this person is "The One."

See also: **Challenge 10:** Having Healthy Conversations

Challenge 18: Agreeing to Disagree

Challenge 23: Staying Yourself when you're with Someone Else

Challenge 21.
Why the Grass Always Seems Greener: How Not to Settle

Sometimes we find ourselves in a relationship and instead of feeling happy, we're plagued by the idea that there's a better someone "out there." If you're experiencing an ongoing feeling that the perfect relationship is right around the corner (but not the one you're in), it's possible you're caught up in "the grass is greener" syndrome. You don't want to settle for less, but it's also important to allow yourself to be in your current relationship. In this section, we go through signs you're thinking "the grass is greener" and what to do about it

1. **Here are some of the signs you might be settling:**

    a. Constantly noticing what is wrong or what you don't like in your partner.

    b. Regularly complaining and being critical.

    c. Always checking out who else might be available (including physically checking out people or on apps).

    d. Feeling bored with your relationship.

    e. Feeling "trapped" in the relationship. This often goes hand in hand with the idea "I have to stay because…. I will never find anyone else or anyone better".

    f. Difficulty making or keeping commitments in the relationship.

g. Expecting everything to be "perfect," with your partner and with the relationship.

h. Focusing on the future of the relationship so much that you aren't enjoying the present.

i. Regularly thinking "What if" or "If only" in regard to your partner.

j. Imagining a different relationship because you don't want to admit you're not happy in this one.

k. Making impulsive decisions without your partner and justifying this by thinking "they won't understand".

l. Doubting yourself, your happiness, or your ability to have a successful relationship.

m. Constantly comparing your relationships to what you see on social media.

2. **Take time for yourself and really consider what you want in a relationship,** as well as the ways this relationship is and isn't meeting your needs (review *Challenge 19: Knowing What You're Looking For*).

3. **It's common, especially in a stressful or difficult time, to have fleeting thoughts about a different relationship.** Allow yourself some time for this to pass, or to see that it's an ongoing theme.

4. **Allow yourself and your partner to be imperfect,** without violating any of your core values or relationship needs and dealbreakers.

5. **Use your journal, or guided breathing, or meditation** to help you think in a clear and balanced way about your current relationship.

6. **If you're constantly comparing your relationships to the seemingly "perfect" ones on social media,** review *Challenge 9: The Dark Side of Social Media.* Keep in mind that social media is only one side of a relationship, and it doesn't reflect what's happening off camera.

7. **If you automatically think of a whole list of negatives about your partner,** challenge yourself to also create a list of what you like, and what works well within your relationship. If the negatives objectively outweigh the positives, it may be time to consider ending the relationship.

8. **Talk about your feelings honestly with your partner.** Use the ideas in *Challenge 10: Having Healthy Conversations* to guide your conversation.

9. **Don't make a decision or act out** before you've assessed what you want from your partner and the relationship.

10. **Trust your gut.** If the relationship doesn't meet your needs, or you "know" you need to leave, pay attention. Make sure you're leaving because this relationship isn't right, not because you're imagining a better one with someone else.

See also: **Challenge 10:** Having Healthy Conversations

Challenge 19: Knowing What You're Looking For

Challenge 23: Staying Yourself When You're with Someone Else

Challenge 22.
Making it Work: If They're not Trying, What are you Doing?

Not every relationship is "The One." It's common to have a number of relationships as you are learning who you are and what you want in a relationship. Occasionally there's immediately a great connection between two people who are able to grow together, but generally relationships are opportunities for learning and discovery. If you're starting to think the relationship isn't working out, here are some steps to take.

1. **Check your perspective.** Ask yourself what you are looking for in a relationship (in general) and then specifically in this relationship. When you think about what you want from a partner, how does your current relationship compare? Think about the words your partner says, the feelings you feel around them, AND their behavior, including whether their behavior is in line with their words?

2. **Are you two on the same page for what you want in a relationship?** If you want an exclusive relationship and your partner wants to play the field, that's likely not going to end well. If you're happy with how things are, but your partner wants to meet your family or talk marriage, ditto. If you know what you want and your partner doesn't — or vice versa — that's also a problem.

3. **Make some lists!** Make a list (or write a paragraph) about the things that are positive and that bring you joy in the relationship. Make a separate list of the things that are bothersome, frustrating or difficult for you in the

relationship. Do these lists look like what you want in a relationship?

4. **Ask yourself how you may be contributing to perpetuating the things that you don't like** — this is an opportunity for you to be really honest with yourself. For example, if you feel like you don't spend enough time together, are you avoiding a direct conversation and giving the "silent treatment" instead of coming up with an activity you might both enjoy?

5. **Consider talking with a close friend or mental health professional about the relationship.** Let them know what you've clarified about what you want vs. what you're getting. Make sure you are open to hearing feedback, and definitely talk about ways in which you may be contributing. Don't take the feedback as criticism; think of it as a way for you to take responsibility for what you truly want and grow into a better person.

6. **Overall, it's healthy to have conversations about what is and isn't working** and to collaborate to determine resolutions. It's difficult to make a relationship work if you're not communicating openly and honestly with each other. This is important especially for the topics that are most difficult to discuss, like sex, money, and respect.

7. **If you want to have a conversation with your partner about how you're feeling, to ask them to make some changes, or to break up,** ask your partner to set aside some time for the two of you talk. Set this up at a place and time that you will have privacy and won't be rushed. Use the guidelines from *Challenge 10: Having Healthy Conversations* and prepare for what you want to say and ask. Remember that you need to be open and willing to honestly listen, not attack or defend.

8. **Be open to compromise and to seeing things from a different perspective,** but don't compromise on your essential values.

9. **Use "I" statements for the conversation** and consider starting with your contribution to what's been bothering you.

10. **If you are just angry or frustrated and feeling like it's "all their fault,"** this is not a good time for a conversation. This is also a sign that the relationship isn't working for you. Before you torpedo the relationship, though, go back and re-assess your contribution and get really clear on what you want.

11. **If there is any form of abuse in the relationship, or any concerns about safety,** skip the conversation and end the relationship. Don't get hung up on "closure" or what the other person deserves. True closure is an internal process of coming to terms with what's happened, your role, and determining how you may handle things differently (or not) in the future. Your psychological and physical safety is the top priority.

See also: **Challenge 10:** Having Healthy Conversations

Challenge 18: Agreeing to Disagree

Challenge 19: Knowing What You're Looking For

Challenge 25: Fighting "Fair"

Challenge 23.
Staying Yourself when you're with Someone Else

Relationships can be wonderful opportunities for growth (and lots of fun!). Relationships also provide an opportunity to learn and experience new things including companionship, romance, and sex. Healthy relationships work best when there's an overlap of interests as well as individual interests.

1. **Make sure that you maintain your own relationships.** It's really important to continue to get together with your own friends and spend time on your own doing things you personally enjoy.

2. **Carve out time for the things you like to do on your own.** Although many couples love spending all their time together, it's important that you take time for yourself too. It's healthy for partners to spend at least a little time apart. If your partner is upset or whines about you taking some time for yourself, that's a potential red flag.

3. **Explore new activities together.** Opportunities to learn and grow together are plentiful. In addition to showing each other your favorite haunts, restaurants, and experiences, it's also fun to tackle new adventures together. You can have fun when you're both exploring. You also get to see how they handle setbacks, unexpected problems, and joy.

4. **Including each other in your separate friend groups is great,** but also make sure that it's not one-sided. If only one of you shares friends, that's not a good sign. Also, if either of you don't like the other's friends, that could be

a problem, especially if it's hard to manage group events or if one person compromises and hangs out together and the other doesn't.

5. **Don't let the "we" outnumber the "I" in your conversation.** As much as you may be in sync, remember you have your own ideas and independence. When you're talking with other people outside of your relationship, allow room for your own thoughts and opinions, not just those of the two of you as a couple.

6. **Compromise goes two ways,** so be generous in your approach and also speak up for what's important to you. Clarify your dealbreakers and your partner's dealbreakers; ensure you're both willing to abide by those.

7. **Continue your journey of getting to know who you are** while you are in the relationship. (see *Challenge 1: Knowing What You Like* for a reminder).

8. **Encourage and support your partner to maintain their individual interests and relationships.**

9. **Make time for the two of you to talk** — not just "catching up" on the day. For example, some people schedule a time once a week or once a month to check and just say, "How is the relationship going for you?" It's also important to talk about significant changes; you or your partner might need some time after big events like a move, a funeral, or a baby, but it's important to come back around and let the other person know how you're doing and what you need.

10. **Treat your partner with respect and compassion.** Always. If you find you're being contemptuous or are having difficulty being respectful, address it quickly.

11. **Don't assume you know what your partner is thinking** (or that they know what you are thinking). Even if you

think you know, check in. Sometimes it's as easy as clarifying your interpretation. For example, "When you didn't contribute to the family get-together, it felt like you didn't really want to do it. Could you help me understand what was happening?"

12. **Keep your sexual relationship vibrant.** Some couples like to stick with what works. Others like to keep things fresh and new. It helps to not assume you know what the other person wants (see #11 above) and to *talk about it*, even if it's uncomfortable at first. Talking about what you like in bed can be sexy too!

13. **Connection matters.** Some couples are asexual or aromantic, and that's totally cool. It's the connection between you that matters most, so nurture that closeness in the ways that work for you.

14. **Remember to continue to engage in loving behaviors**, just like when you first got together. The tender looks, the gentle touches, the sweet "I love you"s all are appreciated any time.

See also: **Challenge 1:** Knowing What You Like

Challenge 5: Engaging in Self-Care

Challenge 24: When it's Not Working

Challenge 24.
When it's Not Working

As awesome as it can be to feel you've found "The One," not all relationships work well or last forever. It's important to look at your relationship clearly, identifying the benefits and the real or potential costs. If you're finding yourself more unhappy than not, here are some of the actions you can take.

1. **Talk to your partner about your concerns** — before they become frustrations, anger, or resentment. This may seem self-evident, but often people try to "let it go" and don't discuss until it's too late

2. **Ensure you haven't lost yourself.** Follow the suggestions in *Challenge 23: Staying Yourself When You're with Someone Else*, especially the ideas about having time for your own interests and outside friendships. Compare how you feel when you're together versus how you feel when you're not together. If you find you tend to feel better when the other person's not around, that's good to pay attention to.

3. **If you find that you are arguing a lot** (especially over what seem to be small issues), consider talking to a mental health professional together. Couples counseling can help you identify what's not working, find common ground, and have more productive disagreements.

4. **Are you or your partner experiencing ongoing jealousy?** See if you can identify the behaviors that bring this up and if there's a reasonable compromise. It could be that one person's behavior is pushing the other person's buttons. Or someone could be up to no good. Recognize the

jealousy when it happens and work to figure out what's behind it.

Ongoing jealousy, or "neediness", are often signs that the person isn't feeling good about themselves. If it's you — try talking to a professional. If it's your partner, this may be a sign that the relationship isn't a good match.

5. **If it feels like you're stuck in a rut or things are boring,** try exploring a new activity together — or better yet, each of you pick something new for you both to try.

6. **Stay away from trying to change your partner or trying to please them by changing yourself.** Compromise is vital, but you each need to stay true to your own values and beliefs.

7. **Look for ways in which you can show (and acknowledge) trust.** Keep your word and expect your partner to do the same.

8. **Be honest with yourself and your partner.** If you've made a mistake, be willing to admit it and take responsibility.

9. **Talk to a trusted friend or therapist** about your concerns to get a more objective point of view.

10. **Treat your partner with respect and expect the same in return.** Ongoing negative or belittling comments are not ok. Review the information in *Challenge 10: Having Healthy Conversations.*

11. **Breaking up can really suck,** but if you're truly not happy or if the relationship involves any kind of abusive behavior, then it's time to end it.

See also: **Challenge 10:** Having Healthy Conversations

Challenge 23: Staying Yourself When You're with Someone Else

Challenge 25: Fighting "Fair"

Challenge 25.
Fighting "Fair"

All relationships involve some conflict at times. It's important to be able to disagree, air concerns, and come to resolutions (or "fight fair") when important issues come up.

1. **Consider agreeing to ground rules.** For example, healthy ground rules can include no hitting anyone or anything, no name-calling and no swearing. Period. If you or your partner can't agree on ground rules, that's a red flag.

2. **Keep in mind that conflict is an opportunity for growth,** so the goal is never to avoid all conflict. If you try to avoid conflict by staying silent or giving in, it generally leads to a bigger blowup later on. Be aware if your partner is doing this and encourage them to tell you what's on their mind.

3. **Talk about one issue at a time and stay on topic.** It's easy to start bringing in additional "evidence" to prove your point, but that ends up coming across as an attack. It's also not helpful to bring up a list of everything you feel your partner has ever done wrong.

4. **Have your conversation in private,** not in front of your kids or your friends or family.

5. **Be respectful in what you say and how you say it.** Not everyone has the same experiences or opinions, and it's very possible you interpret the same information different ways. It's also very possible you didn't realize that something you did could be interpreted differently than you intended.

6. **You don't need to agree, but you do need to listen.** This goes both ways.

7. **Don't interrupt each other.** In addition to being respectful, ensuring each person gets a chance to finish their points, makes sure you each are actually listening and paying attention instead of waiting to respond and prove your point.

8. **Be open about your concerns.** Your partner can't read your mind, and you can't read theirs. Don't expect that they "should" know.

9. **Speak as calmly as possible.** Yelling only escalates the situation.

10. **Use "I feel" when talking about your concern,** not "you." For example, when you start by saying "You ..." it sounds like an accusation, and it probably is. Instead, take responsibility for how you felt.

11. **Stay away from "always" and "never."** It's probably not true, and you risk side-tracking into a fight about exactly how often.

12. **Allow yourself to be curious about your partner's concern or response to you.** Be open to understanding their perspective.

13. **Remember that no one, absolutely no one, is perfect.** That includes both you and your partner. People make mistakes.

14. **Be aware of your own feelings during the conversation,** especially those that may be triggered by the conflict. Take a break if you need to.

15. **Consider ways to negotiate or compromise** unless the conflict is truly against your core values.

16. **Allow the opportunity to take a break from the conversation and cool off.** Do your best to agree beforehand that if things are getting heated, it's time to take a break (and agree to return to the conversation later). Not everyone processes things at the same speed, and some of us need more or less time to consider what happened in a discussion.

17. **Fight sober.** If one (or both) of you has been drinking or using drugs, postpone the discussion until you are both clear-headed.

See also: **Challenge 10:** Having Healthy Conversations

Challenge 18: Agreeing to Disagree

Challenge 24: When it's Not Working

Challenge 26: Taking a Break

Challenge 26.
Taking a Break

You've been in your relationship for a while, and some conflicts just don't seem to be getting better. You're reluctant to completely end the relationship, but the path forward doesn't seem clear. You might want to consider taking a break in the relationship and addressing your individual areas for growth. This doesn't need to be a break like Ross and Rachel (who doesn't love *Friends*?) This means being clear about what you are doing. A break is when you're taking some time apart to evaluate whether or not there's a future in the relationship.

1. **Identify for yourself why you want to take a break.** Do you need time to think; are you feeling that you would rather be alone; are you thinking about someone else? It's important to be honest with yourself about your inner thoughts.

2. **If it's already over, don't ask for a break.** Don't keep hanging on and pretending, and don't try to ease yourself into singledom. That's not fair to you or to the other person.

3. **Discuss your concerns in person.** This isn't a text conversation (and if you know that you really want to end it, then be honest and say that).

4. **Agree to some ground rules for what a break really means**: is there talking, texting, doing things together, dating other people, or not on this break.

5. **Be clear if you are just looking for a day or two of contemplation or if you are wanting something longer.** You

don't have to identify a specific timeline, but there's a big difference between 2 or 3 days and "call me in 6 months."

6. **During your time apart,** allow yourself to do activities or re-engage friendships that may have fallen to the wayside.

7. **Allow yourself time for reflection.** Don't just throw yourself into partying and distraction so you don't feel.

8. **Consider your expectations for the relationship and whether they are realistic and possible.**

9. **Keep a journal to help you assess how you're really feeling** and if you are happier together or alone.

10. **If you haven't seen a therapist,** this might be a good time to consider talking to one as a source of support and to identify additional perspectives.

11. **Take care of yourself.** Check out *Challenge 5: Engaging in Self-Care.*

See also: **Challenge 2:** Identifying Your Inner Voice

Challenge 5: Engaging in Self-Care

Challenge 27: Calling it Quits

Challenge 27.
Calling it Quits

You've tried, and it's just not working for you. Whether this is about core values, your sex life, or general incompatibility, you've decided that this relationship is not "The One." While you're entitled to behaving however you want, calling it quits is a way to further your personal growth. Not all breakups have to be traumatic and terrible and not all relationships have to end up like "the notebook". Here's some ideas to keep in mind.

1. **If you are clear that you don't want to stay in the relationship,** end it. Don't keep hanging on and pretending. That's not fair to you or to the other person.

2. **Similarly, don't ask for a "break" if you already know it's over.** That just prolongs the misery.

3. **Break up in person if at all possible.** This shows respect for the relationship you've had together (and yourself).

4. **Be honest and clear about why you are breaking up.** There's no benefit to making it sound "nice," but don't be mean, either. Find a way to be honest while being compassionate and true to yourself. Of course, if there is any violence, just get out.

5. **State your feelings with compassion.** Whether or not you're both wanting to end it, this is still hard.

6. **Don't lie, or say "It's not you, it's me."** That's avoiding. And trite.

7. **Own responsibility for how you feel** rather than blaming the other person.

8. **Break up in private.** A public spectacle is humiliating for everyone. Of course, if there are any safety concerns, ensure your safety first.

9. **If you're ending it, end it.** Don't keep texting or following them on social media. You are the least appropriate person to console your ex, so stay away. It's also not helpful to judge how they're handling the breakup. Just let it go.

10. **Ghosting is not ok.** You wouldn't want it done to you, plus it's a sign that you're avoiding being your best self. You're allowed to end a relationship.

11. **Stay away from breakup sex.** That's just confusing for everyone.

12. **Find support before, during, and after the breakup.** Ensure you take care of yourself.

13. **If you have concerns that the situation may become volatile or** abusive, consider having the conversation by phone or in public. Safety always comes first.

See also: **Challenge 6:** When You Can't Say "No": Engaging in Healthy Boundaries

Challenge 7: When the Brave Front isn't Enough: How to Know When You Need Therapy

Challenge 28: Whose Is It: How to Divvy Up Property and Assets

Challenge 28.
Whose Is It: How to Divvy Up Property and Assets

As sad or mad or glad as you might be when breaking up, there's still the matter of "stuff." How do you divide your assets?

1. **Contact a lawyer if you have significant assets,** children, or other issues that could make this process complicated. Even if you just have an initial consultation, it will set your mind at ease. If you need to find a lawyer, contact a local university law school for an inexpensive or low-cost referral or Google "best divorce lawyer" (even if you weren't married) with the name of your town and call to ask for a free consultation.

2. **Remember to separate bank accounts as soon as possible.** We always want to assume our ex will behave respectfully, but unfortunately that's not always the case.

3. **Check your state's laws.** If you were married or in a common-law partnership, there may be laws that clarify how assets can be divided. Rules vary state to state. If this applies, contact a lawyer for assistance (See #1).

4. **Identify any major assets that are in both your names and start making changes accordingly.** It might be a while before you can refinance a house or change your car loan, but if you have any assets together, start talking about how to make those work because that will take a while. Until it's resolved, your credit is at risk if the other person does something stupid.

5. **Consider your goal.** Some people have a goal in a break-up of really sticking it to their ex and taking them for everything they're worth. Others have a goal of just dividing things fairly. What is your goal, and how can you stick to that, even when you're upset or hurting?

6. **One way to divide assets is to identify who brought what to the relationship.** Clearly identify what belongs to each person, such as their mother's heirloom dresser or gifts to an individual? Once you have those established, identify out what is not clear, such as music, art, furniture or other items purchased together, or gifts given to both of you.

7. **Consider letting things go.** Identify what's most important and focus on that. Balance the "things" you want to keep vs. the emotional stress and hassle it takes to get them.

See also: **Challenge 6:** When You Can't Say "No": Engaging in Healthy Boundaries

Challenge 10: Having Healthy Conversations

Challenge 31: After the Breakup

Challenge 29.
If Kids are Involved

The hardest breakups are the ones that affect children. It's important to take care of the kids first, which can be difficult when you're not in a good place yourself. It's also another way in which you need to work together with the partner during the breakup. Yikes.

1. **Kids need to come first.** This includes biological children, stepchildren, adopted children, and any other children. Kids are kids, and their well-being needs to be considered and prioritized to the extent possible. Consider where they'll be sleeping, going to school, and seeing friends — and also consider that your ex is still their parent. Always be respectful toward your ex in front of the kids. If your ex is a jerk, your kids will figure it out eventually on their own.

2. **Having kids doesn't mean you must stay together — or that you must break up.** It's not healthy for kids to witness dysfunctional and unhappy relationships, but ultimately, it's up to you and your partner to work through what makes sense for the two of you and what makes sense for the kids.

3. **Kids are resilient.** Many of us grew up in families with divorce and we're fine; many others of us grew up in "intact" families and are not fine. It all depends on so many factors, but a break-up or a divorce by itself isn't going to doom your kid to a terrible life.

4. **Communicate with the kids about what is happening.** It's important to use age-appropriate language and

concepts to ensure your kids know that they are not to blame. Younger kids could benefit from "Mommy and Daddy are going to live apart; we both love you just as much and will spend lots of time together." Older kids better understand divorce or breakups.

5. **Despite the need for communication, some things don't need to be shared with kids until they're older.** If you're not sure about what should be shared with your kids, talk with a therapist. For example, if there was an affair, gambling, addiction, or something similar, a therapist can help you decide if, how, and when to talk about it with your kids.

6. **There are great age-appropriate resources available,** such as the book, "Dinosaurs Divorce," by Laurie Krasny Brown and Marc Brown, which can help kids understand some of the changes happening in their family. A librarian or Internet search can help you find age-appropriate books about divorce. You may also want to read the books to discuss with older children.

7. **Allow children to feel in response to the situation.** Kids react in different ways — they get angry or sad or fearful, they talk back or feel rejected. It's okay for them to have feelings. Keep their safety and behavioral limits in mind (no hitting), but allow them time to work through the changes.

8. **Attempt consistency.** Kids benefit from consistency generally, and during uncertain times it can really help them keep a sense of normalcy. Something like nightly dinners with family, or weekly religious service, or regular visits with other friends or family can serve as a reminder that they are just as loved as always, that time keeps going forward, and that there are good things in the world.

See also: **Challenge 6:** When You Can't Say "No": Engaging in Healthy Boundaries

Challenge 7: When the Brave Front isn't Enough: How to Know when you Need Therapy

Challenge 10: Having Healthy Conversations

Challenge 31: After the Breakup

Challenge 30.
If Pets are Involved

Pets are important to our lives, and in a breakup, we can be more distraught about losing our pet than we are about losing our ex. How do you manage a breakup if pets are involved? Read on ...

1. **Whose pet is it?** If one person had the pet first and brought the pet into the relationship, then the default is that person gets to keep the pet.

2. **Who is the primary pet caretaker?** If one partner knows the vet, the pet's medicines, and where to buy pet food, and the other partner has no idea but likes playing with the dog, it might be worth considering what's best for the pet. Hint: the person who is a better caretaker.

3. **If there are kids involved,** would it make sense for the pet to stay with the kids? It could be a good fit if the kids are bonded to the pet. If children are too young to have bonded with a pet and the pet is very active or high maintenance, it makes sense to split caretaking of kids and pets so one person doesn't get overwhelmed.

4. **What about what the pet needs?** If there is a substantial difference in the partners' ability to provide a good home for the pet, such as a yard for a big pet to run in or someone who travels frequently, it may be that one home is just a better fit for the pet.

5. **Consider shared shifts.** With some pets you can split their time two weeks with one caretaker/two weeks with the other or a similar kind of division. Dogs are often

pretty easy-going about this, but cats are more place-based and might not react well.

6. **Consider visitation.** If both of you are staying local, it might be possible to arrange weekly or monthly playdates with the pet for the non-custodial caretaker. Note this can get awkward when someone gets a new partner or moves away.

7. **You can change your minds.** Pets are generally more flexible than us humans, and if the humans decide one pet plan isn't working, you can try something else.

8. **Don't try to work out your issues through the pet.** If you find that you're arguing more and more about the pet, getting extremely stressed about the situation, or can't come to a conclusion, consider what is most important. You might want to consider changing tactics to come to a reasonable (if temporary) agreement.

See also: **Challenge 6:** When You Can't Say "No": Engaging in Healthy Boundaries

Challenge 10: Having Healthy Conversations

Challenge 31: After the Breakup

Challenge 31.
After the Breakup

Breaking up is hard to do. Aside from the emotional challenges of no longer being with someone, you may also want to move, adjust your financial situation, withdraw from "couple" friends, or completely reassess your life. Although all of these tasks can result in enormous growth, they're not what we would consider "fun."

1. **We don't need to remind you, but breakups can be significant stressors.** This means it's good to take it easy on yourself. Make sure you take care of yourself by eating as healthy as you can, getting enough sleep, moving your body to get out some stress, and talking about things other than the breakup.

2. **Remember it's okay to feel how you feel.** Whether we're the dumper, the dumped, or if it was mutual, we may feel lonely, afraid, sad, rejected, relieved, angry, or despondent. We may feel all of these things at once! However you feel, it's okay. It's also okay if it's difficult to describe how you feel or if others don't agree with your feelings.

3. **Find ways to feel better.** It's ok to take some time and cry, pull the covers over your head, and not deal with the world. At some point, though, you'll have to get yourself back together. You can start slowly, but finding one thing that can make you feel a tiny bit better is a good start. Whether it's a favorite meal or snack, a cup of tea, a good book, watching a game, or getting to work, find something that will help you rediscover the "old you" that has always been in there. Once you find things that help you feel better, keep finding more of them!

4. **Beware of "firsts."** The firsts are the worst. First birthday after a big breakup, first holiday, first anniversary without them, first anniversary of the breakup… for significant relationships, these firsts can feel like breaking up all over again. As the time comes and goes for plans you made together, it's also challenging. Denial doesn't work, but finding other activities to keep your mind and body busy does work. Enlist friends to hang out and distract you, or plan a fun or contemplative day by yourself. The firsts will pass, and then it keeps getting easier as time goes on.

5. **Figure out friendships.** It can be tough to navigate friendships post-breakup. Some couples have friends that are yours, mine, and ours — you may want to stick with your own friends for a while before you navigate friends that you and your ex share. For some people it's also helpful to stick with single friends (if it's too hard to be around couples). Recover, lick your wounds, and then identify how you want to move forward with friends you share. Whatever you do, please don't ask your friends to choose sides or put them in the middle between you and your ex.

6. **Figure out your "in-laws."** If you were close to your ex's family, it can feel like you're breaking up with all of them. Many times, people don't stay in touch with their former in-laws, but you and they (and your ex) can figure out what works for you. If you were particularly close with an in-law before the breakup, it might be awkward at first, but salvageable. Talk it out with your ex if possible, and with the family member too. Be aware you (and they) might need a cooling-off period first so emotions can become less charged.

7. **Work with your family.** Some of us have families who rally around us and support us after a breakup; others blame us for letting go of a "keeper" or say other not-helpful things. You know your family best: set boundaries,

ask for what you need, and if they're not kind, don't share vulnerabilities with them.

8. **Stay in the gray.** It could be tempting to see your ex as the perfect person who got away, or as the awful person who ruined your life. In reality, it's almost never that black and white. If you find yourself romanticizing your ex and the relationship, identify ways in which they weren't perfect, and ways in which you were incompatible. Similarly, if you're full of rage toward your ex, remember they did have some good qualities and you did like each other at one point. As difficult as it is, staying in the gray can help you work through complex feelings, thoughts, and emotions.

9. **Learn from mistakes.** No relationship is perfect, and regardless of how the relationship ended, there are likely areas where you would benefit from self-reflection. Some questions to get you started: What led me to begin the relationship? What did I like most about the relationship? What did I not like about the relationship? How well did I state my needs? What have I learned about myself as a result of this relationship?

10. **Could therapy help?** Some people find post-breakup as a great time to go to therapy to manage grief, make the most of the learning process, or work on healing. Referrals from your friends or doctor could be helpful in finding a good therapist.

11. **Get back in the dating game only when you are ready.** Don't let friends, family, or anyone else (including your ex who found a new someone) pressure you onto a timeline you're not comfortable with. You do you, and you'll get out there again when or if you are comfortable. There's a balance between jumping in with both feet and taking some measured chances.

12. **Know warning signs of a bigger problem.** If you are staying depressed more than a few weeks, drinking too much, feeling like hurting yourself or others, or doing anything else highly risky or dangerous, reach out for help to friends, a hotline, or a professional. No breakup is worth hurting yourself more.

See also: **Challenge 5:** Engaging in Self-Care

Challenge 7: When the Brave Front isn't Enough: How to Know when You Need Therapy

Challenge 32: Dating Again After a Breakup

Challenge 32.
Dating Again After a Breakup

How long after a breakup is a good time to date? There's no one right answer, but here are some things to consider.

1. **"Dating" can mean different things.** If you want to meet up with someone on a dating app for fun, that's quite different than if you're seriously looking for a partner. Messing around or hooking up can be a fun, non-emotionally attached way to ease yourself back into the dating pool, or it can be extremely stressful to even consider! There's substantial variation in what people mean by "dating again," but what's most important is what you mean and what you are comfortable with (see *Challenge 35: Options Beyond Monogamy* and *Challenge 36: Dating and Safe Sex During the Pandemic Era.*)

2. **What's your day like?** If you can't make it through a day without feeling very upset about the breakup, it's too early to date. If you can't make it through a day, you're unlikely to make it through a date.

3. **Think first.** Imagining various scenarios can help you think through how you might feel. Start small and see how far you can go before you want to stop because it's stressful. For example, you can imagine signing up for a dating app, asking someone out, or being asked out. How stressful/sad/exciting does that feel? Pay attention to how you feel. Then consider meeting someone for a coffee date. Or a romantic dinner. Or a kiss ... It's okay if you stop at coffee! Thinking through possibilities first can give you a

good sense of what you're likely to be comfortable with in person.

4. **Dates might feel awkward or stressful at first.** People have all kinds of feelings about dating again after a break-up: they may feel guilty, sad, anxious — or even all three at the same time! Take it moment by moment, and remember you're just meeting up with someone to spend some time together.

5. **What your friends/family think about you dating again is not relevant.** Everyone has an opinion, but whether your mom thinks you should get out there again, or your friends think it's too early, what's most important is what *you* think and feel. If friends or family are pushy with their opinions or pressuring you to date or not date, ask them to back off.

6. **Praise yourself for taking chances.** While reckless or harmful behavior is not a good thing, taking chances and being brave is amazing. Good job! Make sure you praise yourself for being brave.

See also: **Challenge 35:** Options Beyond Monogamy

                      Challenge 36: Dating and Safe Sex During the Pandemic Era

                      Challenge 38: Talking, Hanging Out and Hooking Up

Challenge 33.
Why Am I Not Dating?

Sometimes, we just don't want to date. Sometimes we want to date but can't seem to find anyone. Usually, the most stressful part of not dating is dealing with other people's opinions and suggestions.

1. **What do *you* want?** It's important to understand what you want in the situation. Do you want to date? To find true love? To mess around? To be left alone? Whatever you're looking for, get really clear in what you want, and pursue that.

2. **Manage the input from others.** Everyone has an opinion. Some people share politely only when asked, others share with judgment, and still others really insist you do things their way. When you are clear on what you want, their opinions become easier to manage. Come up with a phrase that works for you to deter them, and repeat as necessary. You could say, "Please stop sharing advice. I'll date when I'm ready" or "Thanks for the advice. What do you think about [unrelated topic]?" or "Interesting.... [and wander off/hang up]."

3. **Talk with trusted friends** who are not going to pressure you. Friends who can listen, reflect, and remind you of who you are (and how amazing you are!) are enormously valuable. If you want, you can clarify what you're looking for, such as whether you'd like someone just to listen or whether you're looking for problem solving. Help your friends help you.

4. **If you're not sure what you want, or if you're distressed with your situation, you may want to visit a therapist.** That's what they're for. A professional neutral party can help you through distress, provide a rational response, normalize your feelings, or let you know if you're off the rails. Whatever it ends up being, you'll be better informed.

5. **If you don't want to date, don't date.** There are plenty of satisfying ways to spend your time that don't involve dating. And anyone who doesn't support you, well, tell them to take a hike.

6. **If you want to date, date.** Whether we're in a pandemic or not, determined people always find a way. You can use dating apps to set up phone or video calls if you can't meet in person. You can commit to one date a week for a month, or a date every day for a year — whatever feels right for you.

7. **... but you can't hurry love.** Getting out there and meeting people will increase your odds of finding someone you click with. But at the same time, if you walk into every date hoping this one's "The One," you're bound to get discouraged. Try to enjoy the process of meeting people and learning more about them and about yourself.

See also: **Challenge 5:** Engaging in Self-Care

Challenge 19: Knowing What You're Looking For

Challenge 38: Talking, Hanging Out and Hooking Up

Challenge 34.
To "I Do" or Not to "I Do"

Marriage is a big step, but not necessarily a required step in your relationship evolution. If you're starting to think about tying the knot, here are some considerations.

1. **What do you want?** Are you looking to spend the rest of your life with someone who makes you a better person? Are you wanting to cross marriage off your list? Are you wanting to nail down a spouse so they never stray? Do you want a fancy party where you're the center of attention? Thinking about what you truly want can be illuminating, and you can identify if those are good reasons to legally connect yourself to someone else.

2. **Why do you want it?** Sometimes people want to get married because they're in love, because they want to raise a family as a committed pair, or because they're determined to spend the rest of their lives together. Others want to end relentless family pressure to "settle down" or feel like they need to settle because they're 30/40/whatever years old. It's really hard to separate ourselves from our socialization that says we're not truly "adults" until we've said, "I do."

3. **What does your partner want?** It helps to be clear on what you want first, but ultimately marriage is a joint decision. Talk about what you want and why. Ask your partner what they want and why. See if you can come to an agreement of "yes," "no," or "let's revisit this." If your partner doesn't want to talk about it, interpret accordingly.

4. **No pressure.** Pressuring someone into marrying you with an ultimatum is never a good idea. Nor are endless delays when your answer is really "no." It may be that no marriage means the end of your relationship, but it's better to face that head on instead of trying to make the other person do what you want them to do.

5. **Consider legal implications of marriage.** Not to dissuade anyone, but marriage comes with legal responsibilities, obligations, and benefits. Joint responsibilities for debt, different tax options, and protection from testifying against your spouse should be explored in case these apply to you.

6. **If you decide to "I do," talk about everything.** Talk about whether you want kids (or more kids), your values, your ways of dealing with friends, your own family, each other's families, money, sex, stress, work, ambition, grief, health, and politics. You don't have to share every deep, dark secret, but do make sure you've at least discussed the most important issues and identified that you can live together. Assume the other person is never going to change and make decisions accordingly.

7. **If you decide not to say "I do," identify how to move forward.** Staying together as partners can happen whether or not there's a ring on it and whether or not you live together. If it's not satisfying to either of you to be living in unwedded non-bliss, though, consider ending the relationship. You owe it to yourself to find happiness.

See also: **Challenge 19:** Knowing What You're Looking For

Challenge 20: Finding "The One"

Challenge 21: Why the Grass always seems Greener: How Not to Settle

Challenge 35.
Options Beyond Monogamy

There are many different kinds of relationships. Most of us were raised with the "ideal" relationship often defined as a heterosexual man and a heterosexual woman in a monogamous, committed relationship that likely included marriage. As they say, we've come a long way, baby! People have all kinds of relationships today!

1. **There are lots of options available.** All of us have our upbringing, moral code, parental/community approval, desires, and other factors to consider.

   a. **Monogamy.** Monogamous dyadic relationships, in which two individuals pledge fidelity and sexual exclusivity to each other as partners, is currently the most popular type of relationship. It's also strongly supported within most major religions as the only morally acceptable choice.

   b. **Monogamish.** Popularized by advice columnist Dan Savage, this is a relationship structure in which two individuals are in a committed relationship and are *mostly* monogamous, with occasional forays into additional relationships under agreed-upon terms (e.g., open communication or no discussion about extra-marital relationships, one night stands only/no emotional attachments).

   c. **Polyamorous.** People can be in romantic relationships with more than one person at a time (e.g., having two boyfriends or a boyfriend and girlfriend). Poly communities help introduce individuals to each other and create bonds.

d. **Open relationships.** Though monogamish leans heavily toward monogamy, open relationships are much more, well, open. Generally open relationships mean that two people are committed as partners but can also be sexually or emotionally non-exclusive as well. Usually partners in open relationships negotiate terms related to communication between partners, emotional connection with others outside the relationship, safety, and other aspects of relationships.

e. **Casual/Friends with Benefits.** This is often another popular option when you aren't interested in being in a relationship but still want to be sexually active.

f. **Swinging.** People in couples who switch sexual partners with other couples or bring single people into the relationship for recreational sex (also referred to as "the lifestyle").

2. **All choices have pros and cons.** We are not in any way suggesting all of these are equally feasible options for everyone. In fact, if you're reading this far, you may already have made decisions about how you want to be in romantic relationships with others. That's all fine. Some people enjoy the opportunity to have romantic relationships or sex with more than one person at a time, whereas others find that immoral, overwhelming, or just not to their liking. Some options come with immediate social approval, whereas others may come with social condemnation.

3. **What you choose depends on lots of things and the value you place on those parts of your life.** As mentioned, many of us were raised that the only option is a heterosexual,

monogamous dyad, and that any other option is unacceptable. Of course, those of us who have come out as LGBTQIA+ may have already upset that apple cart. Similarly, we have religious traditions, our own adult perspectives of morality, parental/community approval, desires, and other factors to consider. As adults we get to decide what we want to bring from our childhood beliefs into our adult present, including whether to meet parental expectations or stay with our religious upbringing.

4. **What about your partner?** It's also worth thinking about how this works out with two people. You may feel most happy when you have the freedom to have sex or relationships with multiple people, but are you okay with your partner having the same freedom? Is your partner ok with you having that kind of freedom? Why or why not? Consider what you'll do if your partner doesn't want to date other people or isn't comfortable with anything other than monogamy.

5. **Whatever you choose, communication is still essential.** Perhaps some people have a fantasy of unlimited sex and excitement with many people while their faithful steady, caretaking partner remains at home. That's rarely what works between two people. That's also not really fair unless both people choose that. Talking about what you like, what you don't like, what you're comfortable with, what you're willing to push boundaries on, and what is off limits is healthy conversation, regardless of what kind of relationship you're in.

6. **Don't forget your desire.** So many people don't pay attention to their desire, and leave it last in their considerations. Especially as young people, desire is important. Think about and explore what turns you on and excites you, and make sure this is a part of your sexual experience.

See also: **Challenge 32:** Dating Again After a Breakup

Challenge 36: Dating and Safe Sex During the Pandemic Era

Challenge 40: Politics between Partners

Challenge 36.
Dating and Safe Sex
During the Pandemic Era

Restrictions due to the COVID-19 pandemic complicate everything, including dating and safe sex. That doesn't mean you need to be cloistered!

1. **Don't freak out.** Many people have lived with very difficult conditions before. Anxiety can be useful in that it can compel you to take appropriate measures to stay safe, such as wearing a mask and washing your hands. Too much anxiety, however, can create paralysis in which you're unable to make any move out of fear.

2. **Clarify your boundaries.** Always a good idea, clarifying boundaries is extra important in pandemic times. These boundaries can include mask wearing, circumstances in which you both take off your masks, willingness to be in each other's living spaces, who else you're willing to interact with, and how much you stick to social distancing. Talk with your doctor or health care professional to get clear on risks and identify what you want to do to stay safe. Be clear on how much anxiety you can tolerate and when you need to dial it back. And consider what to do if someone violates your boundaries — a go-to phrase such as "Whoa! That's not okay!" can be helpful.

3. **The pandemic may upend physical intimacy — get creative!** If you're in an established relationship and both of you are practicing good mask-wearing, hand-washing, and social distancing, your sex life might not need to change

much. For the rest of us, we need to take precautions. At time of writing, it's established that the virus is airborne and is spread through droplets when breathing. It's yet not known the degree to which COVID-19 can be spread through body fluids such as semen or vaginal fluid. For new partners, it makes sense to either quarantine for 14 days or get tested to ensure you're both negative if you want to breathe on each other, such as in face-to-face, unmasked sex. Or you can engage in safer sex by wearing masks and/or gloves, refraining from kissing, exploring non-face-to-face sexual positions, and using condoms or another barrier method to limit the exchange of fluids. If you're not sure, ask your doctor or health care professional what's safer for you.

4. **Be aware that relationships may proceed differently.** "Traditional" relationship progression that starts with deep looks into each other's eyes and progresses to holding hands, then kissing, then more intimate physical contact may need to be adjusted to account for social distancing and safety precautions. Clarifying your boundaries and talking about what you both are comfortable with is a good way to address these differences.

5. **If you're experiencing symptoms of COVID-19 such as persistent cough, fatigue, or difficulty breathing, seek medical care and isolate.** Nothing ruins a new relationship more than one person intentionally or carelessly exposing the other person to a deadly virus. The relationship can wait until you're better.

See also: **Challenge 6:** When You Can't Say "No": Creating Healthy Boundaries

Challenge 32: Dating Again After a Breakup

Challenge 39: Sexting

Challenge 37.
Navigating Social Media: Ego and Etiquette

Twitter, Tik Tok, Instagram, Snapchat all allow new kinds of flirting. Apps such as Tinder, Grindr, match.com, and others let you find people at your fingertips who are down for whatever you're up for.

1. **You don't have to be active on every form of social media.** In fact, you don't *have* to be on any form of social media if you don't want to. Some people link all their accounts so one post goes everywhere. Others stick to one or two accounts and leave it at that.

2. **Whether you use social media for work or for flirting (or both!),** keep in mind that your workplace can review your social media too. You may want to keep separate accounts and keep flirting more private.

3. **To app or not to app.** Some people swear by dating apps, and others refuse to use them. They can definitely be anxiety-provoking, including deciding what to post about yourself, who to reach out to, and who might (or might not) reach out to you. If you approach dating as a competitive sport, where you need to get someone to commit to be your forever partner and spouse, you'll probably have a hard time with apps. If, however, you view dating as a fun way to meet new people whom you may or may not click with, apps could be fun. Either way, always be safe when meeting strangers, and all the other pandemic-safety rules apply here too.

4. **Know your organization's policies about use of social media at work and limit your flirting and swiping at work.** Many organizations track Internet usage on company computers. Do they allow you to check your personal email at work? Are employees allowed to send tweets or update Instagram while on the clock? All activity on company computers and phones is potentially subject to their review, so proceed accordingly. Also, if you are on social media at work, don't assume content is private or will be kept private, regardless of the privacy settings you chose.

5. **Keep your perspective.** Just because you see something on social media, doesn't mean it's true. This applies across the board — to news articles as well as personal posts. Not everyone has the same level of involvement in social media, or uses it in the same way. Go to the source (as much as possible).

6. **Talk with your partner about what's ok and not ok to share.** Some people love to post everything about their life, while others prefer to keep their posting to yummy meals and nature pics. Rather than getting caught off guard, have a conversation about what each of you feel is appropriate and reasonable for posting about your joint experiences.

See also: **Challenge 6:** When You Can't Say "No": Creating Healthy Boundaries

Challenge 9: The Dark Side of Social Media: It's Not About the "Likes"

Challenge 11: Being Labeled a "Millennial"

Challenge 38.
Talking, Hanging Out and Hooking Up

Early aspects of relationships can be challenging in that you're not sure where you stand. You may also have different ideas about where you'd like to end up. It can be challenging to manage your anxiety in these in-between moments. Here are some tips.

1. **Know what you want.** Although it can seem impossible, knowing your values and expectations, what you're willing to do and what you're not, is the most important thing. If you know you're looking for a relationship, then you'll be quick to stop hanging out with someone who's just looking to hook up. On the other hand, if you just want to hook up, someone seeking a relationship won't be the best match for you right now. You could be in a place where you're open to hanging out to see what unfolds. It's okay to want different things, and it's neither good nor bad to want a relationship or to hook up or to see where it goes.

2. **Talking is key.** Talking with the other person is important so you can get to know each other and figure out if you're a good match for what you each are looking for. Even if you are hooking up, you'll still need to have conversations about what you want in bed. If you're pursuing a relationship or just hanging out and seeing where it goes, it can be helpful to periodically check in on how you are doing, and how the other person is doing. Are you comfortable with where things are? How do you feel about how things are unfolding? Do you sense any red flags?

3. **... and so is listening.** Courtship, to use an old-fashioned word, is not necessarily about each person being up front

and direct about what they're looking for. You have to listen to the other person and make decisions from there. Identifying how you feel when you're around them, how much you enjoy listening to them (versus if you're always waiting to jump into the conversation), and whether your values are aligned can be important.

4. **Hanging out is okay**. Sometimes — especially in our 20s and 30s — we get so caught up in "where the relationship is going" that we aren't able to enjoy the moment and just hang out. It's okay to just hang out and see where things go. If you're getting too anxious about where things are going, then it's time to either reassess what you want or have a conversation with the other person — or maybe both!

5. **Hooking up can also be okay**. It's natural for young people to want to explore different kinds of relationships. It's important, though, to be aware of what you want (see #1). You may feel pressure among your friends or from dates to hook up, but if you're not into it, don't do it. Or if you try it and don't feel good during or afterwards, then don't do it again. You won't find yourself in a hookup, so if it doesn't feel good or empowering, or fun, then stop.

6. **Managing anxiety**. There's often a lot of "what if's" as a relationship is unfolding. What if they like me? What if they don't? What if we kiss? What if we don't? This is a good opportunity to breathe and to get more comfortable with not knowing what will happen. In this as in all things, having confidence in yourself that you will be able to manage whatever happens moving forward is key. Of course, if your anxiety is debilitating or interfering significantly with your life, talk to a health professional. For most people, though, it's a chance to learn to manage it better.

7. **Ghosting.** Short answer — it sucks. No one wants to be ghosted. Keep in mind that if someone has ghosted you, they definitely have the issue — not you! (Of course, don't be the ghoster either. It can feel uncomfortable to tell someone you don't want to see them, but it's part of being an adult and having healthy relationships.)

8. **Have fun!** Whether you're heading for marriage or hanging out or whatever you're doing, the path should be enjoyable. Naturally, not every individual moment is heavenly, but overall, the process should be fun. Falling in love is fun! Meeting someone you click with is fun! Enjoy!

See also: **Challenge 32:** Dating Again After a Breakup

Challenge 36: Dating and Safe Sex During the Pandemic Era

Challenge 39: Sexting

Challenge 39.
Sexting

Sexting is sending, receiving, or sharing sexually explicit messages, photographs, or images of oneself to others between phones or computers. Sexting can be fun and exciting, but there are also significant downsides.

1. **Sexting can be a fun way to send messages to your partner or to someone you're interested in.** Sexting can be done as a joke, as a form of flirting, or as a way to get attention. Generally, it's a good idea to start slowly with mildly flirtatious texts and identify where the other person is comfortable or not comfortable.

2. **Like many aspects of sex, the media sends mixed messages.** A simple internet search on sexting demonstrates both "why sexting is bad and harmful" articles and "hot tips for sexting" examples. Sexting can feel empowering but consider implications and consequences before you send anything.

3. **There are significant gender differences in sexting practices — and how sexting is perceived.** Men are more likely to send unsolicited racy photos, and women are much more likely to be pressured into sending racy photos. That said, some men are less comfortable with sharing nudity on the phone, and some women find sexting empowering and flirty. The perception of people who sext is also skewed: women who send nude photos of themselves are considered oversexualized, whereas men are not.

4. **The most important component of sexting photos is consent.** If you're not consenting to have your image shared, or not consenting to receive racy images, then that's not okay, and it might be illegal in certain circumstances. Sharing sexually explicit photos of individuals under 18 can be considered child pornography, as people under 18 are generally not considered able to provide legal consent. Forwarding images without the subject's consent can be considered sexual harassment or revenge porn.

5. **Work phones should not be used for sexting.** If your employer pays for your phone or issues you a phone, they likely have the right to review text messages and images. Don't go there.

6. **Once you send an image, you have no control over where it ends up.** No matter how much you may trust the person you're sending the message to, they may show to their friends, post online, or send to others.

See also: **Challenge 32:** Dating Again After a Breakup

Challenge 36: Dating and Safe Sex During the Pandemic Era

Challenge 38: Talking, Hanging Out and Hooking Up

Challenge 40.
Politics between Partners

Many people choose partners who share their values. Although political differences aren't necessary dealbreakers, some political perspectives may seem or feel incompatible. In a time of red states and blue states, politics between partners can be challenging.

1. **As much as possible, communicate about shared values before you commit.** This includes politics. If you don't have the same politics, that may or may not be a dealbreaker for you. If your politics are different, keep communicating and talking.

2. **Pay attention to the "why" behind the politics.** If someone votes a certain way because that's how their parents always voted, that's a very different situation from someone who has truly researched and looked into the issues. Dig deeper.

3. **If someone doesn't want to discuss politics,** and politics are important to you, consider carefully if you want to move forward. You can let the other person know how important politics are to you, or you can try to approach the issue from a perspective of shared values; either way, it's important to know someone's values if you're going to be partners. If the person won't discuss politics, puts you down for asking about politics, or otherwise responds poorly to your questions, that's not a good sign.

4. **Consider what issues are most important to you.** Some people have very strong opinions on climate change, or abortion, or gun rights, whereas other people feel strongly about different issues. If there are issues that are more important than others,

focus on a discussion about those. Similarly, some of these issues may affect you more directly or immediately than others, such as if you don't agree on whether to keep a gun in the house, or if you have differing views on abortion and are a sexually active heterosexual couple. Keep talking!

5. **Don't expect someone to change.** Just like you don't want them to change you, don't try or expect to change them. Assume they will not change and make decisions about the relationship from there.

6. **Identify any-isms that may be dealbreakers for you.** If someone's political views turn out to be barely concealed racism, sexism, ableism, homophobia or xenophobia, beware. Keep talking!

7. **Figure out what you can and can't live with.** Some couples stick together for decades on opposite sides of the political spectrum. Others break up over elections because they voted for different parties. A person's political affiliation isn't necessarily the most important thing about them. Having conversations about politics is, however, an excellent opportunity to learn about someone's values, empathy, critical thinking, conflict management, and perspectives.

See also: **Challenge 3:** Identifying Your Core Values

Challenge 10: Having Healthy Conversations

Challenge 35: Options Beyond Monogamy

Part 4.
Relationship with Roommates

Challenge 41.
Choosing Roommates

It's challenging to find a good roomie, and relationships with roommates can be challenging because of all the same reasons other relationships are challenging. How do you find a good roommate? Read on!

Special Note: Moving in with a significant other can be stressful (and exciting!). This move falls somewhere between getting along with roommates and living with family — meaning that all of the suggestions in Relationships with Roommates and Relationships with Family generally apply. The difference is the type and degree of emotional (and likely physical) attachment and connection. In the early phases of living together as a couple, it's often easy to imagine that guidelines, negotiations and boundaries won't need to be articulated — you're "in love" and life is grand. Since we know that no one is actually perfect, there will be some problems and pitfalls ahead. Following the guidelines for being a good roomie will help — after all, sharing space is what living together is all about!

1. **Unless you're extremely easygoing, consider carefully who you choose.** It's not ideal to make housing decisions without having substantial conversations about your prospective roommate's values and perspectives. If it's financially manageable, you may prefer to live alone.

2. **If you're planning to live with a friend, consider the potential impact on your friendship.** Is this someone who's awesome for a night out but who tends to

flake on less exciting activities? Do you share a friend group? Make sure you talk through your expectations with each other.

3. **As best as possible, discuss your lifestyle choices.** Does one of you tend to stay up all night, and the other is an early bird? This isn't about judgment, it's about compatibility.

4. **Ensure you have what you need to feel safe.** This can include being on the same page about visitors brought into your house, overnight visitors, and bedroom/bathroom doors that lock. If you discuss these things with a potential roommate who blows off your concerns, do not move in with that person.

5. **If possible, you may want to visit your potential roommate's apartment or home** so you will get a sense of how they live, how clean they are, and what their furniture is like. How does that work with what you have in mind?

6. **If you're couch-surfing or sharing space temporarily, you can be a lot less picky** than if there's a substantial down payment or lease agreement commitment. Consider roommates accordingly.

7. **Ask questions about your roommate's financial situation.** Do they live well above their means? Are they ever late on their bills? Do they take their credit report seriously? These kinds of questions can ensure you find a roommate who shares your values and will protect your credit.

8. **Be cautious if you and your roommate aren't on equal footing.** This can mean if your potential roommate is your boss, owns the home where you'll be a

tenant (or whose relative owns the home), or has a substantially different financial situation. These differences can make it difficult or impossible for you to discuss roommate matters without the better-off person always pulling rank and winning the discussion. That's not a great way to live if you can avoid it.

9. **Check references if at all possible before you move in with someone.** Maybe you have friends or colleagues in common, but ask the hard questions, like how they get along with others, do they argue fairly, and what happens when they don't get their way.

10. **Have a back-up plan.** If somehow things go awry, have a plan for how you can get yourself and your stuff out of the house if you need to, whether to stay with a friend, family member, or someone else. That can give you time to at least sleep safely at night so you can wrap everything up.

See also: **Challenge 6:** When You Can't Say "No": Creating Healthy Boundaries

Challenge 10: Having Healthy Conversations

Challenge 44: Communicating about Cleanliness and Other Stuff

Challenge 42.
Logistics of Agreements

You likely will have two agreements: one between you and your landlord, and one between you and your roommate(s). Understanding what these are about — and penalties if they're not followed — is important.

1. **If you're renting an apartment/house,** you usually sign a lease with your landlord agreeing to pay rent, keep the place in decent working order, call the landlord if there are major problems (e.g., leaks that could damage the floor), and not be a nuisance. The lease will specify how long you're agreeing to stay, monthly rent, what happens if you want to leave early (usually penalties), and circumstances under which the landlord could ask you to leave. People don't usually hire lawyers to review leases, but you will want to read it and ask questions of anything you don't understand. Note that it's a binding contract, so if any landlord says "Yeah, don't worry about that part" cross it out clearly on the lease before you sign, otherwise you are legally held to it.

2. **Agreements with roommate(s) are trickier.** Most times these are not written down, but it could be helpful to get some general agreements in place (and in writing) even without making any kind of formal contract. Here's a checklist of what to consider discussing, before you move in. Note every one of these we encountered with roommate situations:

    a. **Safety.** In pandemic times, it's important to prioritize your safety. How seriously do you and your roommate take social distancing? If you have different perspectives on it, is your roommate willing to be honest with you?

b. **Funds.** Who is paying the deposit? How will rent be managed? Are you dividing the rent equally or dividing differently (e.g., if someone has a larger bedroom)? What if someone is late paying rent? When you eventually move out, how does the deposit get divided?

c. **Utilities.** How will utilities be managed? What if you want different things (basic vs. fancy cable) or use resources differently (long hot showers vs. quick showers) or if one of you has a frequent overnight guest who uses more resources?

d. **Food.** Does each person manage their own food entirely or is there a sharing process? Do you plan to prepare and eat meals together all the time, a few times a week, or only on special occasions? Does anyone have food restrictions or allergies?

e. **Cleanliness.** How do they want to approach cleaning of shared areas? Do you have the same ideas on private rooms (e.g., food in the bedroom)?

f. **Pets.** Sometimes the landlord makes it easy by clarifying "no pets" or establishing a pet fee. If you or your roommate have pets, ensure you discuss how you see that playing out, including whether the pet is allowed in your roommate's room, cleaning standards, and what happens when the pet owner goes out of town.

g. **Guests.** Some people love a busy house; others prefer their solitude. These different types can live together, as long as you both are respectful toward the other. It's also helpful to ensure there's a similar level of drama (low, medium, high) that you both can manage. What's your general agreement on how long girlfriends/boyfriends/friends/family can stay without needing a separate discussion about contributing to the household? And what happens if guests violate rules established? It should be up to the host (not the other roommate) to have the difficult conversation with their guests.

h. **Noise.** Some people can sleep through anything; light sleepers, however, might have challenges if a roommate has friends over late or gets up early for work. If you're both working from home, how will you manage that?

i. **Smoking/Drinking/Drug Use.** If this is something you're sensitive to, if you work in a drug-free workplace, or if one of you is in recovery, this is a critical issue to be addressed. Decide if anything goes, no smoking/drugs allowed, or something else. At least have the conversation.

j. **Handling disagreements.** How do you want to handle disagreements? You've got a lot of options — you could decide to have a weekly meeting to bring up concerns or decide to just bring up stuff as it happens. There's no one right way, but as in everything else, the best bet is to plan how to approach issues when they happen.

3. **How you manage these agreements before you move in together is up to you.** Many people are happy just discussing them and making a handshake agreement. Others want to have a document with all of these in writing.

See also: **Challenge 6:** When You Can't Say "No": Creating Healthy Boundaries

                          Challenge 10: Having Healthy Conversations

                          Challenge 41: Choosing Roommates

                          Challenge 43: Being a Good Roommate

Challenge 43.
Being a Good Roommate

Some people think the best roommate is someone who always pays the rent on time and is never home. Others want a more family-type atmosphere, with several roommates around. Everyone wants their home to feel safe and comfortable — we just have lots of different ideas about what that means!

1. **Be respectful.** Hopefully you've had some time before you moved in to discuss preferences. It's important to respect other people's wishes and preferences, as long as you can still feel comfortable and at home.

2. **Don't badmouth your roommates.** If you're not happy, either keep it to yourself or speak up. Badmouthing roommates never works out well, and it reflects poorly on both of you.

3. **Speak up.** If there's anything bothering you, don't be passive (or passive-aggressive!) about it. Just speak up. It can be as simple as, "Hey, rent's due!" or "Can I talk to you about something? We agreed that ..." Small things can build up over time, so if you know it's something that will keep bothering you, speak up. Starting off communicating clearly will help.

4. **Be flexible.** As Supreme Court Justice Ruth Bader Ginsburg said about marriage, "It helps sometimes to be a little deaf."

5. **Be friendly.** Everyone has good days and bad days. You are not responsible for fixing your roommate or consoling them, but a smile and kind word always helps.

6. **Have good boundaries.** Be aware of what is and is not okay with you, and where you draw the line. Perhaps a roommate eating your chips isn't annoying but taking the groceries you planned to use for a fancy dinner is. Or you're ok with a pet, but you expect any accidents need to be cleaned up immediately. Whatever your line is, be clear, and communicate it.

See also: **Challenge 6:** When You Can't Say "No": Creating Healthy Boundaries

Challenge 10: Having Healthy Conversations

Challenge 18: Agreeing to Disagree

Challenge 44.
Communicating about Cleanliness and Other Stuff

Even if you got everything set up before you moved in, and even if you're best friends, you will still have disagreements from time to time, because you're human. It's so good to have these differences of opinion because you get to practice having difficult conversations and setting boundaries. Yay for learning and growing!

1. **Don't avoid difficult conversations.** If you don't have the conversation, over time you'll become resentful. Which just makes the inevitable conversation more difficult. Nip it in the bud!

2. **A good first step before a difficult conversation is to identify what the issue is and what you would like the resolution of this conversation to be.** Find a way to describe the problem succinctly and ask for what you would like from your roommate.

3. **Consider that we all have different experiences because we focus on different things, and we interpret the same events differently based on our past experiences and our values.** For example, you and your roommate may differ on what is meant by a "clean" bathroom, and you may be proud of your work in a bathroom they find intolerable.

4. **Approach each difficult conversation with a goal of each person getting some of what they wanted.** If you approach as all-or-nothing (you get everything you wanted and they

get nothing), you are much less likely to have productive conversations (or to get what you want from them) in the future.

5. **Demonstrate you are trying to understand what the other person is saying.** Pay attention, nod, or let them know how you are interpreting what they are saying. For example, you could say, "I want to make sure I understand. I think you are saying…?"

6. **Blame is not generally helpful if you're looking for an answer or for a change.** Try to stay away from blame and just stick to the point. "We agreed we would take turns vacuuming the living room, but this place has become a mess. How can we make sure chores get done every week?"

7. **You may want to practice difficult conversations with a friendly partner beforehand.** Anticipate what the other person might say and practice how you might respond to various comments.

8. **Consider the extent to which you let your feelings be involved in the conversation.** Usually it's not personal, even if it feels that way. You can choose to share your feelings if you want. It is important to not let your feelings take over, however.

9. **If you get upset or angry in a conversation,** you can ask for a break or suggest you continue the conversation at another time. That's a better choice than crying or yelling at someone. If you do cry or yell, ask for a break and then go back to the conversation when you're more composed.

10. **Recognize that you will make mistakes** — we all do. Pick yourself up, identify what you learned, and keep going.

See also:

Challenge 6: When You Can't Say "No": Creating Healthy Boundaries

Challenge 10: Having Healthy Conversations

Challenge 18: Agreeing to Disagree

Challenge 45: Roommate Dealbreakers

Challenge 45.
Roommate Dealbreakers

Everyone has dealbreakers. If you're new to living with someone who's not your family, you might not realize how many different ways there are for people you live with to drive you nuts. You also might not quite fully understand that you don't have to put up with roommate situations forever. Knowing your boundaries of what you will and will not accept — your dealbreakers — is the key to managing roommate issues effectively. Here are some common roommate dealbreakers

1. **Drugs/drinking/smoking.** Hopefully you addressed this before moving in together, but if you have different expectations or tolerance for drug use, drinking, or smoking in the shared space, this could lead to problems. Similarly, if one of you gets drug tested for work or is sensitive or allergic to smoke, this could definitely be a dealbreaker.

2. **Destruction of property.** If your roommate or their guest accidentally, or carelessly, or drunkenly destroys any of your property, that can be a dealbreaker. If the property is repairable or replaceable, expect the roommate to take care of the situation and make it right, even if the offender was their guest.

3. **Stealing.** Taking your leftover pizza from the fridge is tough enough. But you have to feel safe and secure in your own space. Get a lock for your bedroom door if you need to, and don't leave your things around where your roommate(s) or others can snag them. If you don't like living like this, start making plans to get out.

4. **Managing guests.** Many roommates are easy-going about guests, but if you find that guests are not following house rules, are disruptive or destructive, or never leave, it's time to talk with your roommate. The general expectation is that you are responsible for your guests. If that's not happening, have the difficult conversation or start thinking about where else to live.

5. **Drama.** Everyone has a bad day from time to time or goes through a slump. But constant drama — breakups, double-crossing, revenge, and sobbing — is enough to make you long for the days when you didn't have a soap opera in your home. If you're getting pulled into your roommate's drama, it's best to stay out.

6. **Pet Care.** If one of you has a pet, that person is responsible for ensuring shared areas are clean, food and water bowls are tidy, pet hair is kept to a dull roar, and any accidents are cleaned immediately. If your roommate isn't taking care of their pet in a way that is considerate, clarify your needs to them and request they start making some changes.

7. **Cleanliness.** The occasional hair in the sink or dishes left out is usually manageable. But if one of you is a neat freak, and the other leaves food out overnight, that could be a dealbreaker. Discuss your expectations, and make sure your distribution of household duties is fair.

See also: **Challenge 6:** When You Can't Say "No": Creating Healthy Boundaries

Challenge 10: Having Healthy Conversations

Challenge 42: Logistics of Agreements

Challenge 46: Moving Out/Ending Shared Living

Challenge 46.
Moving Out/Ending Shared Living

All leases come to an end eventually. You get to decide whether you want to renew the lease or whether one or both of you want to end the lease and find another shared living space or go your separate ways. How do you negotiate this? Carefully, very carefully...

1. **Identify what you want.** Do you want to stay, go, stay with changes, stay under certain conditions? Review what you like and don't like about the space, the neighborhood, the rent, the amenities, the roommate(s), and anything else you have a perspective on. Once you know what you want, then you're in a better position to take action.

2. **Don't blindside your roommate.** If you are sure you want to move out, let them know with at least a month's notice, or more if required by your lease. That is respectful and gives them time to make other plans. Sure, it might be a bit tense in the shared space for a while, but it will pass.

3. **If you're going to stay together as roommates, and switch apartments/homes,** see *Chapter 42: Logistics of Agreements* to review considerations that might be helpful. It will probably be easier now that you've already lived together, but make sure you're on the same page for what you're looking for in a new place, what furniture stays/goes, and how you want to deal with deposits and moving costs.

4. **If you're both leaving the apartment and going separate ways,** it's still helpful to identify whose furniture, dishes, and electronics are whose before moving day so you can

get on the same page with what will happen. Confirm timelines for moving out, how you will handle the deposit, and how you will manage cleaning the apartment to maximize your deposit return. If you're not on good terms, do your best.

5. **If one of you is leaving, review logistics as above** (what's moving/staying, timeline, deposit). Just because one person is staying doesn't mean that all the furniture stays (or goes). Once again, it's all about clear communication.

6. **You may or may not be friends afterwards, and that's okay.** You may leave barely speaking to each other. You may leave as friends promising to stay in touch and somehow never make time to see each other. You may stay close forever. What you can do now is to try to leave on good terms if possible, and then see where life takes you.

7. **Moving is stressful.** There's no question about it — whether one or both of you are moving, there's a lot to think about, a lot of coordination, usually money for deposits or supplies needed, and that creates stress. Do your best to be respectful and to give people extra compassion.

See also: **Challenge 14:** Friendship Dealbreakers

Challenge 42: Logistics of Agreements

Challenge 45: Roommate Dealbreakers

Challenge 47.
Traveling Together

Roommate relationships can be super close or strained. Taking a trip together brings up all kinds of situations you may think you've already resolved. A trip can also be a fun getaway that strengthens your friendship.

1. **Before going anywhere together, talk through everything.** Where are you going? How long will the trip be? How will you handle money? How will you handle disagreements? Make sure you're on the same page as much as possible.

2. **How does your roommate usually handle challenges or difficulties?** Because that's what they'll likely do on the trip, except more intensely. Do they pout when they don't get their way? Freeze you out? Want to talk through everything? Anything you see in your shared space gets even more important when you're in a car or plane together.

3. **What is important to you on the trip?** Be sure you know what you want to get out of the trip. Are you looking for nonstop adventure, a chill time, or to connect with family or friends? Ensure you clarify this to your roommate and discuss how you can handle when you want different things. For example, if you want to relax by the pool and they want to explore, are they ok doing that on their own? If so, awesome! If not, talk it through.

4. **Consider your budgets.** You may have different ideas about what "splurging on a trip" means, whether it means

first class vs. coach or what kind of car rental or how fancy a hotel. Talk it out so no one is surprised.

5. **If one of you has the upper hand financially, consider how this might work out.** For example, if one of you owns the house and the other person is a tenant, how might this play out on the trip? If one of you has the right to kick the other person out of their living situation, maybe a trip isn't the best thing to do.

6. **If one person's family is involved,** consider making sure the other person has permission to be scarce for a while. No matter how lovely one's family is, to someone else, they're still strangers. Understand when one person needs a break, and ensure the one with the family fully supports and runs interference when the other person needs a break.

7. **During the trip, keep talking.** Periodically check in on how it's going. If you're upset or disappointed, say something. If your roommate clams up or seems upset, ask about it. Remember the goal was to have a good time, whatever that means for each of you.

8. **If things go terribly wrong,** consider how this might affect your living situation. How could you coordinate when you get home to either make the living situation manageable or negotiate a respectful parting?

See also: **Challenge 6:** When You Can't Say "No": Creating Healthy Boundaries

Challenge 10: Having Healthy Conversations

Challenge 18: Agreeing to Disagree

Challenge 48.
Politics in the House

Roommates aren't partners, but you can share a lot. What happens when you don't share the same political beliefs? Read on!

1. **As much as possible, communicate about shared values.** Ultimately it may be enough if you and your roommate share values of paying rent on time, picking up after yourself, and being courteous. It's also possible there are hot-button political or values issues that are important to you or that affect your shared space, such as whether you're comfortable with a gun in the house, or what kind of radio shows or media you both listen to. A lot of these issues can be addressed in discussions prior to signing a lease.

2. **Limit political discussion if you're not comfortable.** It's perfectly fine to agree to disagree. You can decide you don't want to discuss politics in the house. For additional tips, see *Challenge 18: Agreeing to Disagree.*

3. **Pay attention to the "why" behind the politics.** If someone votes a certain way because that's how their parents always voted, that's a very different situation from someone who has truly researched and looked into the issues. Dig deeper.

4. **If someone doesn't want to discuss politics,** you can consider dropping it. However, if the person won't discuss politics, puts you down for asking about politics, or otherwise responds poorly to your questions, that's not a good sign.

5. **Don't expect someone to change.** Just like you don't want them to change you, don't try or expect to change them.

Assume they will not change and make decisions about the roommate situation from there.

6. **Identify any-isms that may be dealbreakers for you.** If someone's political views turn out to be barely concealed racism, sexism, ableism, homophobia or xenophobia, beware. Keep talking!

7. **Figure out what you can and can't live with.** Some roommates stick together despite being on opposite sides of the political spectrum. Others argue constantly every election. A person's political affiliation isn't necessarily the most important thing about them. Having conversations about politics is, however, an excellent opportunity to learn about someone's values, empathy, critical thinking, conflict management, and perspectives.

See also: **Challenge 3:** Identifying Your Core Values

Challenge 6: When You Can't Say "No": Creating Healthy Boundaries

Challenge 10: Having Healthy Conversations

Challenge 18: Agreeing to Disagree

Part 5.
Relationships with Family

Challenge 49.
Dealing with Family Expectations

It's natural to have expectations of others, although not all of our expectations are grounded in what is realistic or appropriate. Parents and other family members may have expectations or ideas about you and your life choices that are not in line with your own interests and desires. (And remember, you might have expectations regarding your parents that also aren't realistic or viable). When expectations and actions are closely aligned there's rarely an issue, but when there's a disconnect this can be challenging.

1. **First of all, remember that you're good enough just as you are.** If you need some reminders about this, review *Challenge 2: Identifying your Inner Voice.*

2. **Keep in mind that you are responsible for your own happiness,** which includes who you date, the work you do, the lifestyle you lead.

3. **If you sense that your parents have unspoken, or veiled, expectations,** consider asking them outright about this topic.

4. **Practice using your communication skills when differences of opinion or expectation arise.** There are some good tips in *Challenge 10: Having Healthy Conversations.*

5. **Remind yourself that your parents or family member has their own perspective.** That doesn't mean they are right (or wrong), just that you both have your own point of view.

6. **Assess the expectations that you have for your family.** Are you looking for them to be a universally positive audience? A neutral sounding-board? To provide constructive criticism?

7. **Be clear when discussing your choices or plans** whether or not you are looking for input. Sometimes we are simply looking to share information and other times we are looking for suggestions or advice. If you already know you're in "share only" mode, it helps to be clear about that.

8. **If you've indicated you'd like feedback, then listen respectfully.** If you don't want feedback, gently remind them that you're an adult and responsible for your own decisions.

9. **If you've reached an impasse,** suggest to your parents or family member that this is an opportunity to agree to disagree and change the subject.

10. **Sometimes you may start feeling "heated" or upset.** This is a great time to count to 10 and take a few deep, calming breaths.

11. **It's always ok to take a break from a conversation.** This works best when you tell the other person that you'd like to put the discussion on pause, rather than just walking away or abruptly ending the conversation.

12. **Boundaries are yours to set (and maintain) with family members,** just as in relationships or friendships. You can find reminders and suggestions on this in *Challenge 6: When You Can't Say "No": Creating Healthy Boundaries.*

13. **Talk to someone else** (a trusted friend or therapist) to get some perspective on the situation.

See also: **Challenge 2:** Identifying Your Inner Voice

Challenge 5: Engaging in Self-Care

Challenge 6: When You Can't Say "No": Creating Healthy Boundaries

Challenge 7: When the Brave Front Isn't Enough: How to Know When You Need Therapy

Challenge 50.
Living at Home as an Adult

Over the last decade there's been an increase in adult children living with their parents. Recent research shows that over 30% adults in the United States are living with their parents. As the Coronavirus pandemic continues, this number is likely to continue to increase. While it can be challenging to live with your parents as an adult, here are some ideas on making it work for everyone.

1. **Treat your parents with courtesy and respect.** This is no different than living with anyone else.

2. **Talk about expectations for a timeline before you move in** (this can save a lot of conflict later on). Is this meant to be a short-term situation (for example, it will be six weeks for your new apartment to be renovated and available), or are you imagining that living with your parents is open-ended? If there isn't a specific timeline then generate either some milestones (e.g., once you save enough for a new car) or set a check-in/review time to make sure you're all still on the same page.

3. **Discuss what they are looking for from you** — this may include chores, rent, overnight guests, etc.

4. **If there are differences between your lifestyle and that of your parents,** talk about how you will negotiate this. It's not a matter of right or wrong, just clarification.

5. **Make sure that when you're having these discussions,** you're utilizing all of the communication skills discussed

earlier (*Challenge 10: Having Healthy Conversations* is a good start).

6. **Don't expect your parents to wait on you** (do your laundry, make your meals, etc.). This ties in with your conversations about expectations.

7. **Consider giving your parents a general idea of when you will and will not be home.** This is a matter of respect and good communication, just as you might with a roommate.

8. **Respect your parents' personal space** and ask them to give your space the same respect.

9. **Keep in mind that your parents (and you) may fall into old patterns of interactions or behavior.** This is normal, and it's a great opportunity to practice clear communication.

10. **Plan to have some of your meals separately and some of your meals together.** This allows everyone the opportunity for connection as well as privacy.

11. **In all relationships, small gestures often have great meaning.** Saying thank you, doing an extra chore, or offering to help with something can build a "bank" of positive experiences. This is especially helpful when disagreements inevitably arise.

12. **Start from a positive place.** If you've already got a good relationship with your parents as a foundation, things are likely to go better. If that's not the case, different living arrangements may be a better choice.

See also: **Challenge 5:** Engaging in Self-Care

Challenge 6: When You Can't Say "NO": Creating Healthy Boundaries

Challenge 10: Having Healthy Conversations

Challenge 51.
When Parents have Problems

As humans, we all face difficult times and issues. For some people, this may be a short-term problem. In other situations, such as when a parent has significant mental health or physical health challenge, it can be harder to manage. While you aren't responsible for your parents (and they aren't responsible for you), you may be called upon to assist. Here are some ideas to help.

1. **Stay calm.** This is really advice for everything, but is especially important when your parents are having problems.

2. **Recognize and remember who has the issue and the responsibility.** Often, we feel the need or desire to "fix" a situation, especially when it involves someone important to us. Keep in mind that people are responsible for their own behavior and choices. An example is a parent choosing to not participate in chemotherapy, while the adult child still wants the parent to "fight" the illness. Although you should certainly discuss problematic situations, final decision-making is the responsibility and right of the person with the issue.

3. **Don't take on the role of rescuer.** If you can assist, support or otherwise be of help, that's fantastic. As adults, you also need to meet your own set of responsibilities.

4. **While you may choose to be a primary support**, keep in mind that this is not your obligation.

5. **Do your best to accept your parents for who they are,** even if you don't agree with their decisions or behavior.

6. **Try to talk with your parent about the issue in a neutral manner.** Remember that they have the right to decline talking with you.

7. **Stay away from retaliation,** "fighting back", or telling them what to do. You don't want people behaving this way to you — the same goes for other adults in your life.

8. **Boundaries, boundaries, boundaries.** Know when to say no, to leave a situation, or choose to not engage. This is particularly true if the issue involves conflict between your parents.

9. **Use clear, "I am" statements when addressing the potential impact on you of their behavior or choices.** This is part of good communication. Instead of saying "you always" or something similar, start your comment with stating your own feelings ("I am feeling …").

10. **Have a plan of action that keeps you safe and healthy.** If the situation escalates or involves potential harm, remove yourself.

11. **Remember to utilize your self-care practices.** For a review, See *Challenge 5 Engaging in Self-Care.*

12. **Maintain your support system.** Having friends or a relationship that you can access for support is invaluable.

13. **Consider talking to a professional** — this could be your primary care doctor, a therapist, or a spiritual leader.

14. **Remember, if any situation is really difficult, you always have the right to leave.** There is no obligation to maintain unhealthy or toxic relationships.

See also: **Challenge 5:** Engaging in Self-Care

Challenge 6: When You Can't Say "No": Creating Healthy Boundaries

Challenge 7: When the Brave Front Isn't Enough: How to Know When You Need Therapy

Challenge 10: Having Healthy Conversations

Challenge 52.
Processing Childhood Experiences

While we would all appreciate having a fairytale childhood, for many people this is not their experience. No one is perfect, and no upbringing is without challenges. If your childhood involved trauma or abuse of any kind (physical, sexual, emotional or otherwise), this may still have an impact on your adult relationships.

1. **If trauma was involved,** strongly consider speaking to a mental health professional. While self-help books are great, this may not be sufficient support.

2. **Always practice the basics.** Eat well, sleep well, move your body. This keeps you healthy.

3. **Be willing to name to yourself what has happened.** Often, we try to "push away" or avoid difficult memories, but it's ultimately healing to be able to name and acknowledge what has happened.

4. **Establish and maintain close relationships and a support system.** There's nothing better than having someone to call or connect with when you're feeling down or vulnerable.

5. **Use grounding techniques.** This involves putting your feet on the floor and really feeling the ground beneath you. Alternatively, you could look around the room and name all the items that you see of a particular color (you get to pick the color - make it one you like). This brings you back to the present moment and "grounds" you in reality.

6. **Explore the idea of forgiveness.** This is a gift that you give to yourself. It doesn't mean you condone whatever happened to you. Instead, it's an opportunity to "unhook" your emotions from the circumstances.

7. **Accept yourself for who you** are. You are a complete person, and worthy of love, caring and connection. This is true for all human beings.

8. **Stay away from negative thoughts or replaying difficult circumstances,** to the extent this is possible. Go back to Challenge #1 Knowing what you like and Challenge #2 Identifying your inner voice as a reminder of all you have to offer.

9. **Use slow, deep breathing to help regulate your emotions.** This works for anxiety, anger, sadness — virtually any emotion that you are looking to modulate.

10. **Be honest with yourself about how you are doing,** and be willing to ask for (and accept!) help and support.

11. **If there are toxic relationships that are having a negative effect on your life,** give yourself permission to take a break or step away all together. You have the right to choose what is good for you.

See also: **Challenge 2:** Identifying Your Inner Voice

Challenge 5: Engaging in Self-Care

Challenge 6: When You Can't Say "No": Creating Healthy Boundaries

Challenge 7: When the Brave Front Isn't Enough: How to Know When You Need Therapy

Challenge 53.
Developing Adult Relationships with Family

As an adult, there are major differences in your relationship with your parents, and yet many things may still be the same. Perhaps your parents still live in the house where you grew up, or you may be living with them for a period of time (see Challenge 50: Living at Home as an Adult for some guidance in this area). Whatever your circumstances, you are now in the position of developing an adult relationship with your parents.

1. **First off, it helps to acknowledge to yourself that you and your parents are different people,** and that's totally ok. Although your parents raised you with specific values and maybe specific religious or political beliefs as well, as an adult it's okay to have opinions different from those of your parents.

2. **Keep in mind that your parents are who they are as a result of their own family of origin and life experiences.** This can really help in understanding (and not personalizing) when there are differences in expectations and behavior. One helpful idea is this: people are generally doing the best they can, with what they have, in the moment.

3. **Understand that your parents aren't perfect, and neither are you** — in fact, no one is perfect.

4. **Despite the fact that you will always be your parent's child,** remember that you are now an adult and have the ability (and responsibility) to make your own choices and decisions.

5. **Talk to your parents about your limits and boundaries, and ask them about theirs.** You may think you already know their position, but like you, they've been living and growing.

6. **Just as you don't want them to "change" you,** remember that it's not your job to change them either.

7. **Identify activities that you both enjoy and spend some time with them as equals.** This is a chance for you and your parents to deepen your relationship as adults, beyond the parent/child dynamic

8. **Engage your parents in conversation as you might a work colleague or new friend.** This is the same as in #7. Spend some time getting to know your parents the way you would meeting someone new, rather than believing you already know all about them.

9. **Do your best to avoid unresolved issues or major disagreements from your childhood.** If this does become a topic, remember that you (both) have the opportunity to agree to disagree (see *Challenge 18: Agreeing to Disagree* for more information on this).

10. **If you find yourself engaging in conflict with your parents,** image how you might deal with the issue if it was a friend or colleague. Don't resort to old behavioral patterns.

11. **Don't automatically expect your parents to do things for you.** This is especially true if you are living at home with them. (See *Challenge 49: Living at Home as an Adult* for more on this topic).

12. **If you do start interacting with your parents the way you did as a child, recognize when it's happening.** Ask

yourself if this behavior is reflective of you as a competent, confident adult. If it's not — amend your behavior.

13. **If your parents seem to be reinforcing their role as parents and telling you what to do,** gently remind them that you're an adult and capable of making your own decisions — even if they think your decisions are wrong.

14. **Don't ask your parents for advice unless you are willing to actually hear their opinion.**

15. **Just as in all relationships,** acknowledge when your parents are helpful or do something kind and thank them.

See Also   **Challenge 10:** Having Healthy Conversations

Challenge 18: Agreeing to Disagree

Challenge 50: Living at Home as an Adult

Conclusion.
You've Got This!

We hope you had a good time and learned a few things about yourself and your relationships as you've gone through this book. As we mentioned in the beginning, most people don't go through this book cover to cover all at once. We created this as a "cafeteria-style" guide to answering questions and addressing issues as they present in your life. Keep in mind that all relationships are a work in progress — and that means the relationship with yourself as well! Remember doing the VIA Character survey, or the 5 Love Languages quiz from Challenge 1? It might be fun to review your results and see if your perspective has changed at all (didn't take them? No worries – maybe set aside time to do them soon!) Take a few minutes and use your journal to reflect on what surprised you, what you felt you totally crushed, and what areas you're considering coming back to later.

No matter what — you are worthy and deserving of love, care and compassion, from those around you and from yourself.

You've got this!

About the Authors

Kristina Hallett, PhD ABPP, is a Board-Certified Clinical Psychologist, TEDx Speaker, and Associate Professor of Psychology at Bay Path University with over 25 years of experience working with organizations and individuals. She offers a fresh look at our commonly held beliefs about well-being, serving as a catalyst for change by inviting shifts in mindset, perspective and everyday practices. She speaks internationally in several areas — resilience, radical self-care, harnessing the positive power of stress, and living your best life through self-compassion. Dr. Hallett is the author of two international best-sellers: *Own Best Friend: Eight Steps to a Life of Purpose, Passion, and Ease* and *Be Awesome: Banish Burnout, Create Motivation from the Inside Out*, and hosts the popular podcast Be Awesome — Celebrating Mental Health and Wellness. She can be reached at *www.drkristinahallett.com*

Jennifer P. Wisdom, PhD MPH ABPP, is an author, consultant, speaker, and principal of Wisdom Consulting. As a consultant, she helps curious, motivated, and mission-driven professionals to achieve their highest potential by identifying goals and then providing them with the roadmap and guidance to get there. Jennifer created the best-selling *Millennials' Guides* series, including *Millennials' Guide to Work, Millennials' Guide to Management & Leadership, Millennials' Guide to the Construction Trades,* and *Millennials' and Generation Z Guide to Voting*. Dr. Wisdom is a licensed clinical psychologist and board-certified organizational psychologist. She has worked with complex health care, government, and educational environments for 25 years, including serving in the U.S. military, working with non-profit service delivery programs, and as faculty in higher education. She is an intrepid adventurer based in New York City and Portland, Oregon. She can be reached at *www.leadwithwisdom.com*.

Made in USA - Kendallville, IN
1232974_9781954374003
02.15.2021 1212